THE CENTERFOLD SYNDROME

GARY R. BROOKS

Foreword by Lenore E. Walker

THE CENTERFOLD SYNDROME

How Men Can Overcome
Objectification and
Achieve Intimacy with Women

Jossey-Bass Publishers • San Francisco

Substantial discounts on bulk quantities of Jossey-Bass books are available to corporations, professional associations, and other organizations. For details and discount information, contact the special sales department at Jossey-Bass Inc., Publishers.
(415) 433-1740; Fax (800) 605-2665.

For sales outside the United States, please contact your local Paramount Publishing International Office.

TCF Manufactured in the United States of America on Lyons Falls Pathfinder Tradebook. This paper is acid-free and 100 percent totally chlorine-free.

Library of Congress Cataloging-in-Publication Data

Brooks, Gary R.
    The centerfold syndrome: how men can overcome objectification and achieve intimacy with women / by Gary R. Brooks.—1st ed.
    p.   cm.—(The Jossey-Bass social and behavioral science series)
    Includes bibliographical references (p. 213) and index.
    ISBN 0-7879-0104-0
    1. Men—United States —Sexual behavior. 2. Heterosexual men—
United States. 3. Sex (Psychology). 4. Intimacy (Psychology). 5. Man-woman relationships—United States. I. Title. II. Series
HQ28.B76   1995
306.7'081—dc20   95-8838
                                             CIP

FIRST EDITION
HB Printing   10 9 8 7 6 5 4 3 2 1

Calvin R. Brooks

1922–1993

He did all he possibly could

CONTENTS

FOREWORD

The women's movement, which began in the late 1960s and continues today, has fundamentally changed the way women and men relate to one another. Nevertheless, old habits die hard. More significantly, some deeply conditioned attitudes still have a profoundly negative impact on both individual identity and the potential for intimate relationships between the sexes.

In this book, Gary Brooks offers a way to overcome one of the most insidious and destructive of these conditioned attitudes: men's objectification of women's bodies, their voyeuristic preference for perfect trophies over real women, their secret masturbatory images that invade their minds not only on the street but even while making love to their partners, isolating men in their own fantasies.

Dr. Brooks calls this malady the Centerfold Syndrome, since its most obvious symptom is a fixation with the pursuit of those airbrushed fantasies from the pages of *Playboy* and *Penthouse* magazines. But the social conditioning that has created this obsession can be found everywhere in our culture: on television, in advertising, and in the way men are raised. They are brought up to both depend upon and yet also resent the power they perceive women hold over them as gatekeepers to this precious commodity—their objectified body parts!

Gary is painfully honest about many men's blighted concepts of sexual relations. But he goes beyond mere analysis to document a group of his patients who are both abusers and victims of the Centerfold Syndrome. You will see George confronted by his own daughter, who wants to be a cheerleader in a skimpy costume. You'll meet Arthur, who is dealing with his wife's mastectomy—first put off by the disfiguring surgery, then able to get beyond these feelings to recognize his emotional bonds to her after so many years together. You'll also follow the real-life drama of Chad, who struggles to have a real relationship with a "plain" girl after dozens of unsatisfying one-night stands with "babes . . . big breasts, long legs, hot-to-trot." And Mike, obsessed by the compulsive use of pornography for masturbation. Not to mention Paul, expelled by his wife, who finds a young and gullible surrogate woman to abuse. These and other members of Dr. Brooks' group fight to overcome the ingrained attitudes and habits of the Centerfold Syndrome and to achieve some kind of real partnership and intimacy with women.

Ultimately this is a positive book. Its message is that change is possible, that many men and women have the desire to improve the way they relate to each other, to move, sometimes in a painstakingly slow crawl, toward the expression of emotional intimacy and sexuality. Many of the men in this book are well on the way to becoming the partners of new, feminist women. They will be the ones who design the new rules for relationships.

This is an exciting time to live in, and this book gives us good ideas about how men and women can live together with a greater sense of intimacy and true partnership.

June 1995   Lenore E. Walker

PREFACE

Among the many things that are right and admirable about contemporary manhood, there are some things that are not working well at all. Most men struggle resolutely to meet the continually shifting expectations of the male code. For the most part, their efforts produce vital benefits for their loved ones and for themselves. In some ways, however, everyone gets cheated. This book is about one of those ways.

The Centerfold Syndrome looks critically at the sexuality of heterosexual American men. Much of what I describe will apply equally to gay and bisexual men, but I am most confident in my knowledge of the heterosexual male population, so I have restricted my observations to this group.

My thesis is that there are a number of ways in which the traditional construction and practice of male sexuality are highly dysfunctional. Most men are too voyeuristic, too objectifying of women's bodies, too competitive for sexually attractive women, too needy of validation through sexuality, and too fearful of emotional intimacy. As I will attempt to demonstrate, it makes sense to conceptualize these problems under the rubric "the Centerfold Syndrome."

As yet, I can't provide scientific evidence that the behavioral patterns I have observed fit neatly into one syndrome, or that they are part of several problem configurations. I can't be certain that others have observed similar patterns. Only research and public discourse can clarify this. What I can say with some certitude is that there clearly are significant problems with heterosexual male sexuality and that these problems make it very difficult for women and men to establish emotionally intimate relationships and to experience sexually gratifying lives.

In the following pages I will describe my observations, my formulations about these observations, and my ideas about what needs to be done. This should be interesting.

Temple, Texas   Gary R. Brooks
June 1995

ACKNOWLEDGMENTS

An interesting and stimulating symposium presentation never would have evolved into this book if it had not been for the vision and enthusiasm of my editor, Alan Rinzler. He knew immediately what I was trying to say, helped me refine my message, and pushed me relentlessly to complete the project. Nothing less would have worked.

For the twenty-three years during which I have been a professional listener, troubled men have taught me invaluable lessons about the stresses of manhood, forever dispelling the naive idea that only clients benefit from the adventures of therapy.

Like so many men who are trying to find a new path, I am deeply indebted to many courageous and compassionate women who have offered ideas, critique, challenges, and compassion. A brief list must include Michele Bograd, Glenace Edwall, Phyllis Frank, Lucia Gilbert, Roberta Nutt, Carol Philpot, Louise Silverstein, Barbara Wainrib, and Lenore Walker.

Because I once thought I traveled alone, I have been elated to discover the friendship and encouragement of many caring men. Ron Levant, Don-David Lusterman, and Roy Scrivner have been mentors, teachers, and most-treasured friends. Joe Rickard taught me how to be a professional. Joe Pleck has been an intellectual beacon. Many other men—Bob Brannon, Jim Doyle, Glen Good, Richard Lazur, Jim O'Neil, Ron Ruhnke, Murray Scher, and Jack Sternbach—have helped me explore new ways of being myself in the company of men.

My mom has always given tirelessly of herself and made me want to be the most I could be. My dad fought his entire life, and in the process gave me courage to face my fears.

My daughters, Ashley and Allison, have given me joys I couldn't have imagined. Patti has been a loving and supportive partner, who has made the journey easier and the future bright.

—G.R.B.

THE CENTERFOLD
SYNDROME

1

WHAT IS THE CENTERFOLD SYNDROME?

I'm a relatively normal and emotionally stable guy who grew up believing that looking at and desiring physically attractive women was both pleasurable and inevitable. Now I'm not so sure.

During the past several years, as I have studied the lives and conflicts of men, I have begun to question the value of much of what I had previously accepted. I once assumed, as many men do, that success at work and in a career was the greatest measure of a man, that physical toughness and heroic acts were pathways to proving manhood, that men had to keep the upper hand with women, that only "queers" loved other men, and that emotional sensitivity and vulnerability were signs of weakness. Of all these assumptions, however, none has been more deeply ingrained than the belief that physically attractive women's bodies are the most magnificent spectacles in nature, and that men are destined to fervently desire them, to compete for them, to sacrifice emotional and physical well-being for them, but rarely to enjoy them except from afar. Men and women have accepted this bizarre state of affairs, strangely enough, as both unavoidable and relatively harmless. Neither is true. In fact, in studying this situation I have come to the conclusion that this male pattern of relating to women's bodies, which I am calling the Centerfold Syndrome, represents one of the most malignant forces in contemporary relationships between men and women.

The centerfold has been one of the dominant cultural icons of the past half-century. As interpreted by *Playboy* magazine's founder Hugh Hefner and *Penthouse* magazine's publisher Bob Guccione, today's centerfold is a racier, slicker, and glossier fantasy woman, even more perfect and idealized than the pinup girl of the 1930s and 1940s. Her airbrushed perfection permeates our visual environment and our consciousness, creating unreal fantasies and expectations, imposing profound distortions on how men relate with women and to women's bodies, and, in turn, how women relate to their physical selves and with men.

ELEMENTS OF THE CENTERFOLD SYNDROME

The five principal elements of the Centerfold Syndrome are (a) voyeurism, (b) objectification, (c) the need for validation, (d) trophyism, and (e) the fear of true intimacy.

Voyeurism

Nothing heightens the emotional intensity of a sexual encounter as much as looking directly into the eyes of one's partner. Similarly, the unique features of a female partner's physical appearance—the way her breasts swell in a dress, the outline of her torso through gossamer fabric—can become a powerful sexual stimulus for a man. Certainly, the visual sense always has and probably always will play a major role in men's sexual responsiveness. In the latter half of this century, however, this component of men's sexuality has been so exploited, distorted, and outrageously exaggerated that the emotional and sexual health of most contemporary men has been seriously compromised.

Throughout our culture, in movies, on television, in magazines, and in public meeting places, men are continually assailed with images of naked and semi-naked women. Not only are the glossy soft-core porno magazines more plentiful than ever, but even the covers of many "women's" magazines feature the same type of comely, buxom models who are also pictured on hot rod magazines, tabloid newspapers, and, once a year, mainstream sports magazines. Advertising billboards promote "men's clubs" that are "topless" or "bottomless" or that feature models in lingerie. A popular restaurant celebrates women's "hooters" more than it celebrates its food. Beer companies seem to be competing to see which can cram the most bikini-clad women into a thirty-second commercial. Superhero comics are liberally sprinkled with images of breathtaking superwomen in skintight bodysuits. The creative inspiration for one entire television series is the adventures of scantily clad lifeguards. Increasingly, women are encouraged to wear bathing suits and exercise outfits that cover their derrières with little more than a thin fabric strip.

Only religious fundamentalists and radical feminists appear to be alarmed about this wave of female body glorification. The culture at large seems to be generally indifferent to this trend, seeing it as harmless titillation, pretty much a natural product of men's biological makeup. I strongly disagree with this position. It is my contention that this mania, this explosion in glorification and objectification of women's bodies, promotes unreal images of women, distorts physical reality, creates an obsession with visual stimulation, and trivializes all other natural features of a healthy psychosexual relationship.

Objectification

Voyeurism and objectification are closely related. Just as the Centerfold Syndrome calls for men to become *observers*, it also calls for women to become the *observed*. Women become objects as men become objectifiers. As the culture has granted men the right and privilege of looking at women, women have been expected to accept the role of stimulators of men's visual interest, with their bodies becoming objects that can be lined up, compared, and rated. The process is distinctly one-way, with women's bodies highlighted and male observers remaining in the shadows or anonymous in a crowd. Objective physical aspects are critical: size, shape, and harmony of body parts are more important than a woman's human qualities. The women objectified by the media remain relatively anonymous, often without names, except for pseudonyms such as Miss May, Miss Nevada, or Miss Rotary Camshaft. Despite the occasional pretense of connection through shallow interviews or background sketches, centerfold women are left devoid of real personalities, portrayed as superficial cartoon characters. Men talk of their attraction to women in dehumanizing terms based on the body part of their obsession—"I'm a leg man," or "I'm an ass man."

What's more, one fantasy woman is never enough, since images that initially can be enormously novel and exciting can quickly lose their zip. Objectifying observers soon find one naked woman boring and routine, and look for new and different images to provoke their fascination—"variety is the spice of life." At times, the confirmed objectifier becomes so attached to the thrill of the new and different visual experience, he resorts to the kinky and the offbeat, becoming preoccupied with visual fetishes. Bizarre magazines featuring only "Big-Breasted Mamas," "Black Beauties," "Oriental Cuties," or "Biker Babes" are in part a pathetic effort to override the boredom inherent in such superficial sexuality.

Since centerfold fantasy women are presented only to stimulate and to invite admiration of their perfection, they are unlike real women, who not only have physical flaws but also expect things from relationships and can be interpersonally threatening. When centerfold women are available to men as visually perfect and emotionally distant sexual fantasy objects, real women become more complicated and less appealing. In fact, when men become fixated on narrow and idealized images of female beauty—youthful bodies with uplifted breasts and full but firm bottoms—their real partners, by comparison, may come to be seen as not only less appealing but even ugly. Stretch marks, varicose veins, sagging breasts, and cellulite-marked legs, common phenomena for real female bodies, may be viewed as repugnant by men who see women as objects.

Furthermore, when a man in a relationship is continually distracted by a fantasy life dominated by visual images of idealized bodies of strangers, that man will frequently be emotionally absent from his partner; he will be unable to have intense, here-and-now experiences with her. Tragically, if he spends most of his emotional energy on sexual fantasies about inaccessible people, he frequently will not be available for even the most intimate emotional and sexual moments with the most important person in his life.

The Need for Validation

The traditional concept of manhood is an elusive state to achieve. Most men have only a vague sense of their masculinity and, therefore, continually worry about whether they measure up, and they are quick to become alarmed at the first sign of failure, weakness, or vulnerability. They are programmed to crave validation of their masculinity, and they frequently view women's bodies as a medium for that validation. This need for validation disempowers them and creates an odd yet vitally important inversion of the traditional power relationship between women and men. Despite the fact that they generally have had considerable advantages over women in physical strength and economic and political opportunities, men have frequently felt one-down about sexuality. Although there are multiple ways that women could conceivably validate a man's masculinity, the avenue critical to most men is the sexual one. When women are envisioned as sexual objects and made the centerpiece of men's visual world, they become imbued with enormous psychosocial power. They are seen as having invaluable manhood tokens that they may, or may not, choose to dispense. The more physically attractive a woman is, the more validating power she is seen to have.

What have made matters worse are the long-standing gender differences in socialization about sexual activity. Young men have been encouraged to be promiscuous—that is, to seek sexual activity with scant consideration of relationship needs, intimacy, or emotional compatibility. At the same time, young women have been encouraged to attract men's attention, yet to withhold and serve as the gatekeepers of sexual activity.

Even when participating in sex, men are not free from the need for validation. In recent years, thanks to abundant technical advice from sex manuals and implicit assumptions that men's "performances" are the critical determinants of sexual fulfillment, many contemporary men have become obsessed with producing physical evidence of women's sexual pleasure. A dramatic response from a woman's body—erect nipples, gyrating hips, a shuddering orgasm—can be interpreted by a man as unambiguous evidence of his manliness. Conversely, a cold, listless, or indifferent response from a woman's body often leaves a man feeling ineffectual, inadequate, or resentful. Rarely can a woman find the right words to reassure a man of his worth when he has decided that her body is underappreciative of his manly attentions. To many men, the state of a woman's body may come to be viewed as a masculinity barometer, with its natural fluctuations mistaken as irrefutable evidence of either a man's sexual competence or his shameful inadequacy.

The power imparted by women's sexual leverage, when viewed in light of women's relative powerlessness in other spheres, sets the stage for considerable misunderstanding between women and men. Women, of course, are keenly aware of men's economic and political leverage, but are frequently unaware of the degree to which men feel powerless in terms of sexuality. Men, aware of their insecurities about sexuality, are deeply fearful of women gaining power in areas once thought to be the basis of men's security and worth.

At this critical juncture in the history of gender relations, the Centerfold Syndrome is made infinitely worse by a culture that plays to men's fears and heightens men's feelings of sexual disempowerment. As I have already discussed, artificially enhanced images of exquisitely desirable women are everywhere, but these women are remote and unattainable. They are on screens or glossy pages, but physically unavailable. They parade across well-lit and well-guarded stages, before masses of sexually aroused men who hoot but don't touch and are ultimately left unfulfilled, frustrated, and demoralized.

All men and all women are diminished by this noxious situation. The very few women who meet centerfold standards only retain their power as long as they maintain perfect bodies and the leverage of mystery and unavailability. All other women suffer from pressures to live up to the outrageous centerfold standard and from the disappointment of partners when they fail. The very few men who form sexual relationships with centerfolds are often left disappointed, fearful of loss, or envious of those who tryst with even more desirable centerfolds. The great majority of men who never come close to sex with their dream woman are left feeling cheated or unmanly.

Trophyism

Men also experience their masculinity in relation to other men. That is, they ask themselves, How do I stack up against the other guys? Men compete in this way because they believe that the tokens of masculinity are in short supply, with the most valuable prizes obtained by only the worthiest men. Women's bodies become part of this scenario as they are objectified and treated as potential trophies—living testaments to a man's prowess as a financial success, skillful sexual performer, or fearless warrior.

This male competition for access to women's bodies begins in adolescence when boys compete to be the first to "score," to achieve the most sexual conquests, to "make it" with the sexiest teenage girl. The women's-bodies-as-trophies mentality, damaging enough in adolescence, becomes even more destructive in adulthood, when the "trophy hunts" of adolescence clash with men's developmental need to "settle down" and select a long-term companion. While collecting new and different sexual trophies may be celebrated among male adolescents, it is a sign of emotional immaturity in the world of most adults. Furthermore, while actual trophies retain their basic physical characteristics, human trophies do not. Women's bodies age, losing their trophy-like characteristics, especially in comparison to newer varieties. Hence, the trophy-hunting man, initially satisfied with his trophy-wife, must eventually face the maddening reality that his prize will eventually lose her lustre, while other potential prizes will emit near-irresistible allure.

Another aspect of this trophyism mentality makes it especially dangerous. Trophies, once they are won, are supposed to become the property of the winner, a permanent physical symbol of accomplishment and worthiness. This cannot be so with women's bodies. Women, of course, no longer want to be passive objects, and they have a growing say in who they spend their lives with. From the perspective of the trophy hunter, this is a horrifying trend, as he can never be assured that his trophy will remain his. At any time, she may choose to sit on the shelf of another man. This is a devastating occurrence for a trophy-hunting man, one that commonly provokes him to desperate and destructive reactions.

The Fear of True Intimacy

Men are created within women's bodies and their first experiences of love and security come from intimate physical contact with their mothers' soft and welcoming bodies. Fathers' bodies could provide similar sensual pleasures, but they traditionally have been unavailable to young boys, or when available, have been stiff and threatening.

Though young boys treasure the opportunity to be physically close, both for sensual pleasures and for reassurance in times of vulnerability, they soon encounter social pressures to distance themselves from their mothers' bodies and establish a place alongside the bodies of men. This early developmental injunction, endemic to traditional parenting of boys, causes them to have lifelong conflict with women's bodies, a conflict that is the essence of this fifth and most complex aspect of the Centerfold Syndrome.

Young boys are conditioned to feel shame over feelings of weakness and vulnerability, encouraged to suppress their needs for sensual physical contact, and expected to develop male body armor with hard muscles and an emotionally stoic exterior. While they try to emulate heroes that are brave, intrepid, fearless, physically aggressive, and emotionally tough, boys cannot ignore that they are still insecure and crave physical comforting. At especially vulnerable times, they may allow nurturers to give some measure of soothing and comforting, but fears of humiliation quickly surface. Frequently, boys discover that some touch and physical closeness are possible through acceptable "boy" activities like sports and horseplay, but they remain continually aware that these sensual pleasures must not be acknowledged.

In short, boys learn to associate women's bodies with softness, intimacy, and sensuality, the very qualities they have been taught to reject. Despite their common exteriors of manic activity and rough play, boys often crave physical closeness and sensuality, but have no way to ask for it and few avenues by which to experience it.

In adolescence, young men find themselves besieged by two powerful yet contradictory forces—waves of sexual urgency and the extreme prohibitions against emotional intimacy. The sudden appearance of the hormonal pressures of sexuality catches young men unprepared; the fear of intimacy leaves them confused and conflicted. Help is rarely available. Usually there is some token guidance in the form of caution about the need to be sexually controlled, but boys recognize these admonitions to be contradicted by their bodies, their peers, their role models, and their culture, in which the dominant message is that sex is great and a man should acquire as much of it as possible.

Sadly, young men, who have had minimal preparation for the multiple complexities of sexuality, have also been encouraged to be physically tough and insensitive to emotional issues. Emphasis has been placed on aggressive and competitive skills, with very little emphasis on interpersonal skills of communication, empathy, and nurturing. Young men badly want sexual intimacy, but have learned to fear and suppress their needs for emotional intimacy and sensuality. They learn that the safest form of sex is the "slam bam thank you ma'am" variety.

It is conceivable that under optimal circumstances sexual activity might help boys to rediscover these long-suppressed parts of themselves and might help them unlearn their fears of these "feminine" qualities. The opposite typically occurs, however, as young men experience their brushes with sensuality and emotional intimacy as confusing and threatening to their hard-won masculine independence and desire for "sexual freedom." Most young men therefore give primacy to their sexual needs, while continuing to suppress their needs for sensuality.

As young men learn to wall themselves off from too much emotional intimacy in sex—to develop nonrelational sexuality—they are also taught to sexualize all feelings of emotional and physical closeness. As a result, they become unable to experience nonsexual intimacy. Because their closest approximations of emotional intimacy and most intense exposure to sensual pleasure occur almost exclusively in the context of rapid-orgasm sexual activity, male adolescents learn to closely associate sex and intimacy. Further, they are poorly tutored in distinguishing the two, because they have been raised in a culture that generally gives minuscule attention to men's sensuality and intimacy needs while exalting their sexual needs. Because of this confusion, it should not be surprising that a man who wants to replace his feelings of emotional distance and alienation with ones of closeness and connection misinterprets the feelings as sexual ones and assumes that he is just "horny." Consequently, men may seek sex when they really want emotional intimacy, sensual pleasure, or physical comforting. Moreover, they frequently may engage in sex when they have no interest whatever in emotional intimacy.

Sometimes the distinction between the desire for sex and the desire for intimacy is irrelevant. In some cases, a sexual relationship may help a man discover his sensuality and intimacy needs, and he may develop a deeply fulfilling relationship with his partner. More often than not, however, this blurring of sexual needs and intimacy needs will create significant relationship constraints. When young men do not learn to distinguish the two sets of needs, they will be highly restricted in their capacity to develop and maintain relationships. For example, intimacy with male peers will incite homophobic panic, and intimate friendships with girls will be contaminated by compulsive sexual overtures. Limited in their pursuit of true intimacy, young men may be prone to overdependence upon a sexual partner; or to defend against excessive intimacy, they may seek promiscuous sexual activity, rather than risk getting too close to a partner. Even when remaining monogamous, young men may be prone to seek distance through fantasy and emotional withdrawal.

Ultimately, this fifth aspect of the Centerfold Syndrome is about how men are taught to suppress their needs for intimacy and sensuality, and come to invest too much emotional and psychological power in some women's bodies. Fearing their potential overdependence on women, men develop a preoccupation with sexuality, which powerfully handicaps their capacity for emotionally intimate relationships with men and for nonsexual relationships with women.

WHY AREN'T THERE MORE COMPLAINTS?

Although the tenets of this syndrome are indoctrinated into children at an early age, some of the teaching has been so subtle that the more covert implications are missed. Commonly, the

Centerfold Syndrome is accepted as a relatively natural outgrowth of innate, gender-based biological differences. Furthermore, the social and psychological tension produced by the syndrome has often been presented as culturally beneficial—the basic lifeblood and energizing force of our society. The significant problems related to the syndrome have been disguised or dismissed.

Consequently, only some women have protested as yet that the Centerfold Syndrome objectifies them, depersonalizes them, reduces them to body parts, perpetuates anatomical lies, and idealizes unreal fantasies about women's bodies and sexuality. Sadly, many more women accept some of the fraudulent premises of the Centerfold Syndrome and take on the hopeless task of meeting its standards, rarely satisfied with their successes, and ultimately blaming themselves for the inevitable failures.

Yet, although damage to women as the result of the Centerfold Syndrome is gradually becoming clear, there is virtually no awareness that it also harms men. This isn't surprising, since very few men seem dissatisfied with their sexual socialization. Most seem happy to embrace the Centerfold Syndrome, though some will admit disappointment that they have not been able to capture a true centerfold. Nevertheless, it's my contention that the Centerfold Syndrome is deeply harmful to women *and* men. It produces major asynchronicity between men and women and is a crucial component in the "battle of the sexes." Since it prevents real intimacy, mature discourse, and honest interpersonal connection, it creates barriers to understanding and becomes a significant obstacle to healthy relationships.

The Centerfold Syndrome is pervasive, but it is not inevitable. It is neither an unavoidable outgrowth of biological forces nor the product of moral weakness resulting from Adam succumbing to Eve's temptation with the forbidden fruit. Rather, it is a social construction, and like all socially constructed realities, it can be deconstructed.

A BRIEF MEMOIR

My experiences as a man have provided me with an essential resource for appreciating and conceptualizing the psychological issues of the Centerfold Syndrome. So, before launching into a description of the clinical situations that inspired this work, let me introduce some of the relevant personal experiences that shaped me as a listener to the life stories of male clients.

Early Years

Even as a kid, I liked looking at attractive girls or women. I wanted to do it all the time—even when it was inconvenient, awkward, or potentially embarrassing. For example, I can remember times when driving around (or in my younger years, riding on my bike) I'd go past a particularly attractive young girl in shorts or halter top and risk an accident through my efforts to visually follow her in my rearview mirror as she walked in the opposite direction. Fortunately, there were other settings, like the beach, that were especially conducive to girl watching, as they allowed for random and unpredictable movements. Unfortunately, the best views occasionally required entering frigidly cold and otherwise unappealing water or risking sunburn waiting for a girl to shed her towel to get down to serious sunbathing.

The efforts required to watch girls' bodies were frequently a pain in the butt. Furthermore, they seemed kinda weird or sick. I might have tried to give them up if it wasn't so easy to dismiss them as innocent, harmless, and generally healthy examples of an old cultural tradition—that is, standing on the corner watching all the girls go by. After all, didn't the guys and I entertain each other with stories about the many ingenious ways of stealing glimpses of girls' bodies? As depicted in the movie *Porky's*, we never tired of inventing tricks such as dropping pencils to look up skirts, shining patent leather shoes for their reflective abilities, lurking at the base of stairs to view girls ascending, or finding perches to look down blouses at bras or cleavage.

But something never seemed right about this enormous fascination of staring at young women's bodies, or more accurately, at female body parts. Of course, there were some rationalizations. One seemed obvious: we stared because that's what guys do, that is, women are the natural objects of men's desire. The survival of the species depends upon women turning men on and men seeking to procreate with those women who visually stimulate them. That made some rudimentary sense, but didn't really capture the flavor of our interest. I mean, procreation never really seemed that important; in fact, avoiding it seemed a lot more important. In most cases, we fellows didn't want to sire offspring; we just wanted to get a better look at those marvelous bodies beneath those sexy clothes, and, to be truthful, I guess you could say that we wanted to touch, rub, and fondle as well.

Over the years, I heard another explanation that seemed somewhat less primitive: women's bodies are among God's more beautiful creations and, in the tradition of the great master artists, one should appreciate them as a sort of aesthetic exercise. This sounded like a far more appealing rationale for this activity, but this explanation didn't lack problems. For example, if we guys were such lovers of natural beauty, why did we spend hours ogling women and virtually no time with other objects of "natural beauty" such as vibrant sunsets, colorful birds, or delicate flowers? Why weren't we equally fascinated by other male bodies? Furthermore, the emotional and visceral experience of suddenly coming upon a "stunning" woman was quite different than that of other aesthetic activities, as it usually was anything but calming or relaxing. Admittedly, some have described confrontations with great art or natural beauty that can "take your breath away," but the confrontations with physically desirable women seemed far more unsettling, disquieting, and disruptive. Few of us left a visual encounter feeling that we had been uplifted or had reached a transcendent sense of peace. Rather, we would feel turned on, excited to the point of distraction, sometimes "so horny we might explode."

Now, this seemed truly peculiar. Everybody seemed to endorse the idea that visual lust was natural and enjoyable, yet in retrospect, many of us were really experiencing that visceral response as, at best, a mixed bag. We felt no interest in minimizing the ubiquitous exposure to sexual images, and usually were relentless in seeking as much stimulation as possible, but the ultimate objective was not to develop an intimate relationship, or even an emotionally intimate moment, and the ultimate outcomes were generally painful and frustrating.

Even the most enthusiastic champions of the joys of visual lust had to acknowledge that the practice had an uneasy compulsive quality. We felt a hypnotic pull that was almost irresistible, regardless of the moment or the stimulus. It didn't seem to matter what we were doing or what we were trying to focus on. If a sexy girl walked by, appeared bikini-clad in an inane beer commercial, or partially exposed her breasts on a magazine cover at a grocery store checkout counter, we had to drop what we were doing and look.

The Mysteries of Male Sexuality

One might think that since girl watching was such an emotionally draining experience, guys would spend considerable time talking about it, questioning its value, speculating about its causes, wondering about alternatives. This was far from true. Although I can remember countless hours spent talking about beautiful female bodies, I can't remember a single conversation in which any of us seriously questioned the inevitability of girl watching. It would have been nice to have had a forum for open exploration of this and many other aspects of our lives, but asking questions and sharing insecurities was not a big item among my young male friends.

Even though our sexual desire for young women was one of the central issues of our adolescent lives, we never really felt that it was acceptable to admit ignorance or express curiosity. I knew practically nothing about sex, sexuality, or my own emotional and physical makeup, let alone that of young women. I had a wealth of partial information and misinformation, but I was never sure exactly what I knew, what I needed to know, or whom to ask if I was ever able to formulate a straightforward question. Sexual ignorance wasn't a valued commodity, but sexual expertise, even when feigned, was something that would impress the other guys.

Sex education therefore became a peculiar sort of detective work—observing and inferring, without permission to ever ask direct questions, check out theories, or clear up inconsistencies. The best strategy seemed to require that we should study the guys who seemed to be experts, who seemed to have some bravado or sense of confidence about the whole process. Since the loudest and most outspoken guys, generally known as "studs" and "cocksmen," were considered the "masters," we usually learned about women from them, the guys with the biggest sexual compulsions and most dedicated to worshipping female bodies and "chasing pussy."

Lessons from My Dad

Of all the men who taught me the "benefits" of looking at women, none was more influential than my dad, who was himself one of the most striking incarnations of a man infected by the Centerfold Syndrome. My father not only loved to look at women, but unlike some men, he loved to do it conspicuously. He loved to talk about women, women's bodies, and anything sexual, so much so that most people considered him to be one of the most sexually preoccupied persons they had ever encountered. He was one of the original inspirations for the phrase I came to detest: the guy with the "one-track mind." Unfortunately, the description was apt, as his life seemed to be governed by sex. My dad collected *Playboy* and other girlie magazines and kept them within easy reach. No attractive woman could pass by without comment and no sexual innuendo or chance for sexual double entendre would be overlooked.

The blatancy of my father's behavior was mortifying to my deeply religious and socially sensitive mother. While it was embarrassing to me, in truth it was simultaneously intriguing. Sure, I was troubled by his need to embarrass my mother, and I wanted to impress my mother with my Christian virtues. Yet I too was affected by the irresistible pull of beautiful female bodies. Though I really wanted to be the pure and virtuous person I thought my mother wanted, and though I really tried to pretend not to notice, I couldn't ignore my own carnal reactions. Though I avidly tried to become like my mother, I had to admit that a part of me was very much like my dad. Inside I knew that we shared a bond—a powerful and irresistible urge to look at women's bodies.

This made for a tricky situation. In my mother's presence I tried to appear aloof and superior to my father's crude sexuality. But when he and I were together, we could enjoy our shared pleasure since, strange as it was, this shared addiction was always a source of potential closeness for us. If I ever wanted to get my dad's attention, or have a shared moment with him, all I had to do was bring his attention to a woman's body, and we could admire her together.

Hanging on the Corner with the Guys

My adolescent social life was spent primarily with a tight group of guys that regularly met at a central street corner in our neighborhood. Though we didn't always spend our time there, we knew it to be the point from which all activities were launched. The corner was more than a meeting place, however; it was also a place of life transition. That is, it held more than geographic significance. It was known in the community as the place where guys grew up. During the period that any group of guys occupied the corner—and the corner saw many groups come and go over the years—it was the center point of the group's identity, the locus of life education, and the site of transition from adolescence to rudimentary adulthood.

Although there was no body of accurate information to be shared, nor a logical system for ascertaining who really knew anything, we guys spent considerable time teaching others what we thought we knew. In general, the teachers were those with the most credibility as experts and the greatest need to impress others. In terms of women and sexuality, the experts were the ones claiming the most sexual experience and proficiency. As experts, we could be quite generous in sharing our tales of sexual mastery, requiring only an attentive audience willing to accept our claims without questions and ready to endure our mockery of any revealed ignorance, although everyone of course feigned sexual sophistication. Admittedly, all of us we were skeptical of one another's claimed expertise, but we were thrilled to have some break from strictly monitored public conversations and to find a forum for addressing the pressing issues of women and our seemingly uncontrollable lust.

In these private all-male situations, it was pretty easy to get other guys talking about women's bodies. In fact, debating the talent of various sports stars, the relative speed of various cars, and the comparative value of various women's bodies was our principal mode of interacting. Once again, there was a major difference between how we talked in public, or when women were around, and how we talked in private. In public we revealed our sexual preoccupations far less than we experienced them; in private, we actually may have given them greater attention than they warranted, since in some peculiar fashion, talking about women's bodies was one of the few ways for us to feel safe communicating with each other. As with my father, I found that obsessing about women's body parts gave my male friends and I one of the few safe avenues for emotional connection with each other.

This bonding came at a high price, however, since the conversations were hardly open, but rather were relatively constrained. We always exaggerated, embroidered, and embellished, never revealing weakness, insecurity, vulnerability, ignorance, confusion, or failure. In our ubiquitously competitive style, we struggled to match the feats of our sexual heroes, outdoing each other in reporting sexual conquests, exaggerating at points, and inventing entire stories when necessary. Sexual defeats such as having advances spurned or having pickup lines rejected were cause for group ridicule; a girlfriend leaving for another guy was cause for profound humiliation. If such rejections became frequent, the guy not only had no chance of sexual heroism but also risked taking on the permanent identity of a real sexual "loser," a wimp, or chump, since "some guys have it and some guys don't."

In that era, a prominent sexual hero for many of us was James Bond. Although he wasn't the first idealized "womanizer," Bond, played by Sean Connery, captivated me and my peers. Secure, confident, and utterly competent, he seemed to have an insatiable appetite for casual sexual relationships with gorgeous women. Without the slightest difficulty, he was able to seduce any woman that didn't come on to him first. The women were identical: visually striking, sexually preoccupied, and unavailable to all other men. The "relationships" were sex based, with no evidence of emotional intimacy, commitment, or even compassion for a partner's welfare. Some affairs lasted a few scenes, but none were carried from one movie to the next. Often, the target of Bond's sexual interest was a "double agent," and the sexual relationship was actually an act of war. As strange as it is to imagine now, at that point in my life I was enthralled by Bond's aplomb at attracting, captivating, and when necessary, replacing these beautiful women. I imagined that if I somehow could master his detached and aloof style, I could have similar "success" with women and be envied by other guys.

This male peer group was quite unforgiving and intolerant of sexual inadequacy, but that wasn't the only problem. In addition to being an omnipresent threat to my personal esteem, the group was also problematic as a perpetuator of sexual misinformation. No one really knew much of anything about sex. What little we knew was about sexual mechanics, generally gleaned from magazines and porno movies. Knowledge of relationships and emotional needs of women was nonexistent; but since ignorance was shameful, we tried to portray ourselves as experts. For example, almost all of us had some awareness that a woman's "clit" (no one knew how to pronounce clitoris) was a key component in female sexual gratification, but no one really knew where it was located, let alone how it fit it into the larger context of a woman's sexual and emotional response. We sort of had the idea that any nonviolent method of "getting to her clit" was likely to produce sexual melting of a woman's resolve and lead the way to sexual conquest. These posturings would have been comical if it were not for the lasting damage done by these charades.

Although our rap sessions were heavily laced with celebration and adoration of Mary's incredible hooters or Lisa's unbelievable ass, these sessions were in many ways quite upsetting. Amid the male bonding and joint celebration of the joys of catching glimpses of naked women, or in extremely wonderful cases, of actually getting to touch or fondle them, was the reality that our most intense desires would very rarely be fulfilled. We were continually stimulated, teased, tantalized, yet almost always denied and frustrated. We would be bombarded by unrelenting images of women we would desperately desire but never touch. Surely, we thought, these women knew this. Probably they did it on purpose and enjoyed the reactions they stirred in us.

What was rarely admitted was the degree of our desperation, confusion, and feelings of powerlessness. Women had phenomenal power to stimulate and excite us, making it totally impossible for us to focus on anything else, yet they seemed to get sadistic pleasure and interpersonal leverage from withholding fulfillment of our desires. It wasn't hard to tap our resentment over the actions of women as "prick teasers"—those women who specialized in provoking us with provocative displays of nipples, butts, and crotches through tight clothing. At its most hostile, this all-male adolescent environment was a fertile ground for misogyny (fear and mistrust of women, which will be discussed further in Chapter Four) and tacit support of rape.

It is now painful to admit, but at some of our most frustrated moments, almost all of the guys felt a small secret sympathy for the horrible images of men getting revenge on unattainable women. We tolerated and at times even thought the unthinkable, saying things like, "I'd like to fuck her till she hurts," "to come in her face," "to fuck her in the ass," or "to see her get gang banged." Almost all of us to some degree came to endorse the view that for the time being the only reasonable accommodation to the problem of powerful attractive women was to stay in control by limiting our contacts to sexual ones, since these seemed to allow us to keep the upper hand and avoid the darker dangers of deeper and more sustained relationships.

Looking for a Partner

It would have been nice if the fifteen to twenty thousand hours we spent in bull sessions analyzing women, women's bodies, and sexuality ultimately had produced greater understanding of the social environments we were about to enter. It would have been nice if those hours spent with the guys had provided deeper understanding of the complexities of our own psychological makeup. Ideally, this understanding could have provided confidence in who we were as young men, so that we could then learn more about the truths of young women, producing an integrated view of male-female realities.

We never came close. As I reflect on that period of my life, I remember intense and passionate, sometimes almost desperate rap sessions, repeated nightly, sometimes into the early morning hours, for several years. And then it ended. Silence. There were no more opportunities to get together and share frustrations and passions.

I'm not sure why it stopped. Probably because we had to "get on" with our lives. Probably because these sessions had outlived their usefulness and weren't accomplishing anything.

Whatever the reason, without these encounters we lost the opportunity to eventually get it right. If we had continued to meet, we might have used them to analyze new information from the worlds of marriage and relationships, and ultimately developed a more balanced view of women, women's bodies, and sexuality.

The transition from the intense male world of adolescence into the world of dating and heterosexual relationships probably took place gradually, over several years. Yet in retrospect it seems that the change came about abruptly and somewhat prematurely. One day we were getting together for "pussy talk," sharing our strong ambivalent feelings about women. The next day, it seemed, we were immersed in an intergender world, having little appreciation of our confusion or of our need to figure things out. Naturally our resentments, hostilities, and general distrust of women didn't disappear; they just went underground.

My years after leaving the corner were characterized by a confused mixture of seeking sexual adventure and seeking emotional closeness, as I had no clear idea of what my relationship needs were. I missed getting together with the guys. Even at their most frustrating, the meetings had always provided security, companionship, and a sense of identity. I wasn't sure where to go from there. Short-term, superficial sexual relationships certainly had their attractions—new bodies to touch, feel, smell, and experience—yet these encounters became increasingly disagreeable and unfulfilling. It was bad enough to realize that relationships based on sexual desire alone would inevitably disappoint, but it was more unsettling to experience the inexplicable depression, the vague sense of emptiness that they invariably seemed to generate. I wouldn't want to go through it again.

Today, it seems to me to be no great mystery that these sexual encounters, often based on motives no loftier than the desire to see and touch an interesting female body, would be unsatisfying. But then it was puzzling. In a few years, increasingly weary of these encounters and longing for something more substantive, I was forced to face my ambivalence about long-term relationships. How badly did I want one? Was I ready to abandon the James Bond fantasy of perpetual sexual adventure seeking that had held such crazy fascination for my friends and me? How ready was I to let go of the centerfold mythology? I opted for relationship seeking, but I am embarrassed to admit, not without some psychic wrestling.

Having decided to take on the complicated task of seeking a more meaningful relationship, I encountered further problematic residuals of adolescent ideology, and I encountered the centerfold mythology. One nutty concept was the idea that a guy's worth is measured by the physical attractiveness of his partner. An unattractive partner (a "hound") was a disgrace. It may have been marginally acceptable to briefly or covertly date a hound for sexual exploitation, but extended contacts made a guy a target for ridicule. Similarly, some latitude could be given for a marital partner, since nurturing and caretaking abilities were also granted to be important; but a guy's wife still had to be physically appealing. What is more, since theoretically his wife's body might be the last one a guy would experience, there had to be some significant degree of physical attractiveness to compensate for the loss of variety.

Further complicating matters was a general distrust and fear of "gorgeous" women, whom men tended to view as shallow, self-centered bimbettes. They couldn't be trusted, partly because we expected them to be the target of every horny guy in the world. This clearly created a conundrum, as the perfect mate had to achieve some balance between being just attractive enough to compensate for the loss of access to other women's bodies, yet not so attractive to be threatening. One commonly repeated phrase reveals a great deal about our odd state of mind. "The woman you marry should be someone you are proud to show off before the guys, but aren't ashamed to take home to mother."

My first serious relationship had little chance for success, to some extent because I entered it while my values were in transition. When I met "Sharon," I was getting ready for a more mature relationship, but I was still too much a captive of the Centerfold Syndrome. Driven primarily by voyeuristic needs, I found a girlfriend who was quite attractive, but much too young, naive, and inexperienced. Although we were an abysmal match in many areas, we each provided something the other was seeking. I was sexually aroused, and assumed that the other needs would somehow fall into line. Sharon wanted a serious relationship, someone to love, and seemed to assume that sex was a natural part of that equation. Not surprisingly, this relationship ran into serious problems as my sexual fascination vacillated, my impatience with her "shortcomings" increased, and our differing agendas became more apparent. I felt unfulfilled in most areas except sexual ones, yet to my discredit, I continued the relationship for many months, finding it hard to let go of the occasional sexual gratifications.

There were other relationships and other problems, many of them attributable to my continued fixation in the Centerfold Syndrome. "Anita" was bright, intellectually stimulating, and passionate, but too thin. One or two girlfriends were quite attractive, but still had unforgivable physical imperfections. Sadly, I now realize that no relationship could have worked, since even if someone met my absurd physical criteria, I couldn't have met her criteria for emotional maturity. I was far too caught up with the need to seek new and different confirmations of sexual virility. I was sick with the need for validation of my masculinity. What is more, I was heavily into competition, and sexual conquests were still too important as tokens of progress up the hierarchical ladder of male status.

By the time I met Patti, my wife, I had matured some. I seemed to have less need to prove myself through sexual adventures. I still wanted an attractive wife, but also a partner who was intelligent, fun, compassionate, nurturing, and socially competent. Patti seemed to be all of those things, and we quickly developed a very serious relationship.

It would be great to report that all traces of the Centerfold Syndrome had magically disappeared by the time we married and that our relationship has never been affected by it. That, of course, is absurd; the truth is that I've needed lots of time, lots of intense self-examination, and lots of patience from Patti, to make significant progress.

I have continued the struggle against the symptoms. At times I have grieved for the loss of the sexual adventures that are possibilities in the single life; I have envied men with more centerfold-like partners; I have wished that partners wouldn't age; and I have pressured Patti to be physically more, physically less, or physically different. Sometimes this has created significant tensions, but we have survived with a quite solid relationship.

Entering Professional Training

My education about the Centerfold Syndrome continued when I entered a graduate training program in psychology, but not in the ways that I had anticipated. Perhaps because I'd associated psychology with Freud, I expected graduate training to be abundant with study of and discussions about sexuality. More than one observer has suggested that people entering psychotherapy training are at least partially motivated by a desire to work out their own issues. I wasn't an exception to this, since I'd hoped that graduate training would give me ideas about managing my reactions to women's bodies. In part, I expected to discover a learned community of thoughtful and self-disclosing men who would openly describe their struggles with sexual lust and provide tips on how to put these issues into appropriate context.

What I encountered was quite the opposite: I generally found the men in graduate school to be pretty cautious, guarded, and reserved, far more reluctant to talk about personal struggles than my adolescent peer group. Though this initially took me by surprise, I quickly adapted by silencing myself and taking on a more passive observational stance as I tried to decipher the ground rules of this new environment.

What I began to sense was discouraging: graduate school would be totally about studying the problems of *them*, the patients/clients on the other side of the one-way mirror. Implied though not clearly stated was the assumption that as professional men in graduate training, we had worked through our adolescent confusions and were now prepared to engage women colleagues and clients in the most emotionally intimate settings without the remotest possibility of interference of misplaced sexual arousal.

As I listened to what male colleagues did and did not talk about in their descriptions of their cases, I was led to believe that at most they'd had minor adjustment difficulties in managing sexual feelings toward female clients. In fact, it appeared that if sexual feelings were aroused in a therapy session, the responsibility was assumed to be the problem of the "seductive" female client, not the problem of a male therapist with unfinished business in the area of sexuality. This situation made me tremendously uneasy. Where had these guys developed such maturity around attractive women? Where had I been when they'd worked these issues out? Many of them had had considerably more personal therapy than the meager amount I'd had—perhaps that explained it. Admittedly, I was in a far better place with this issue than I'd ever been before. I had a gratifying emotional and sexual relationship with Patti, but I certainly hadn't been able to completely turn off all visceral reactions to the bodies of attractive women. In part, I was embarrassed and ashamed to admit my immaturity, my continued inability to move beyond adolescent sexual urges. Since I badly wanted to be a responsible psychologist, I vowed to suppress these desires and avoid any further discussion of them. This helped, for a while. Once I stopped talking about this source of discomfort, I stopped getting uncomfortable reactions, I stopped feeling like a misfit, and I began to be accepted as a mature professional-in-the-making.

It wasn't until many months later that I began to make a new discovery: there were cracks in the armor of some of my male colleagues. All of them were not as fully comfortable with sexual issues as I had originally thought; they simply were better able to hide their feelings. Over time, at unguarded moments, they revealed their conflicts, either through subtle comments or transparent humor. Additionally, I was fortunate to develop close friendships with other young men in training, friendships that permitted deeper revelations and sharing of common concerns. To my relief, I learned that I was not completely alone, that other fellows shared many of the same conflicts.

From Graduate School to Professional Roles

By the end of my fourth year of graduate school, I had become more comfortable with the new world of educated men, and more distant from the coarse and unrefined world of my adolescence. I had learned about theories of human behavior and psychopathology, and I had learned a new language to describe human interaction. I hadn't resolved my issues about voyeurism, objectification, and lust, but I had been able to put those issues aside. In fact, except for continued participation in sports, I had pretty well moved away from many of my ties to traditional men. This wasn't easy for Dad, who frequently would ask sarcastic questions such as "Well, how does a man of your educated position feel about this issue?"

My graduate school years, during the early 1970s, were contiguous with the early phases of the contemporary feminist movement, and this had additional impact on my interactions with women. Though I hadn't yet grasped the full implications of feminism, I had enough sense to realize that the traditional sexualized modes of relating to women would bring nothing but trouble. This was a perplexing time for many of us guys. New ways of being a man were being demanded. We were being expected to develop greater interpersonal sensitivity, compassion, and respect for women as equals. Surrounded by bright, assertive, and competent women, we recognized that this was no environment for the Centerfold Syndrome—treating women as sex objects was a sure ticket to professional hell.

But had the syndrome really disappeared? Had we completely exorcised all visceral reactions to physically attractive women? Had we eliminated all voyeuristic needs? As an adolescent, I had realized that exceptionally attractive women made most all of us men nervous; but what about attractive women who were also bright, assertive, and competent? The Centerfold Syndrome in this setting had intimidating implications.

It seemed to me that professional women in professional settings were being treated in a fashion quite different from how women were treated when I was an adolescent. By and large, they were not treated as bodies or sex objects; their competence and intellect were respected. I assumed that this change was largely an outgrowth of feminist pressures and a product of more enlightened men (including myself). Maybe we had developed a high level of psychosexual maturity. Maybe the Centerfold Syndrome was a relic of the past.

But there were disquieting signs. If one watched closely, certain residual symptoms could still be observed. It sometimes seemed that for some men in power positions, physically attractive women had an advantage over their less physically attractive peers when it came to training positions, research opportunities, and teaching assistantships. When senior male professionals developed questionable relationships with their former students, generally the physically attractive ones were singled out. Very attractive women still seemed to evoke strong reactions in professional men, even if the reactions were disguised, muted, or denied. Case conferences about sexually attractive female clients often revealed subtle anxieties in male therapists. *Playboy* magazines were still being read, and sexist jokes were still being told, although usually out of earshot of certain female colleagues.

I left graduate school eager to get started in the practice of psychotherapy and enthusiastic about the role of psychologists in changing people's lives. Intoxicated with my newly discovered psychological wisdom, I wanted to help others come to appreciate the value of interpersonal sensitivity, self-awareness, and gender equality.

Through a series of peculiar circumstances, my initial job was in a Veterans Administration (VA) hospital, a strange setting for a Vietnam-era peace activist. The transition into working in this system should have been easy for me, and probably would have been if college and graduate school hadn't gotten in the way. I had grown up in a traditional blue-collar male setting, and at one point in my life I'd had much in common with the typical VA patient. I knew firsthand about their most pressing problems, insecurities, and values, but I had spent several years in an educational system that taught me to conceptualize these people from a culturally neutral framework. I had learned to think about these men as psychological entities, and had developed the requisite emotional distance and scientific objectivity. In doing so, I thought of them intellectually, suppressing the emotional connection we shared. I tried to lecture to these men, dominating the therapy sessions, pointing out the foolishness of their actions, trying to hammer home the superior values of new age masculinity.

Interestingly enough, in spite of my messianic zeal, I couldn't help but be moved by their stories, their confusion, their plight in a rapidly changing world. As I began to listen more and talk less, I recognized our similarities, and began to reflect on my own adolescent struggles. In drawing on my own background, I found an avenue to empathic connection I had previously missed. I began to help these men clarify what they were thinking, to put confused feelings into words, and to discover poorly recognized sources of

anger and frustration. I found that my psychologically framed interpretations were commonly greeted with "Doc, you just don't have
the capacity to understand what we're going through"; but when I
drew on our common experience as men, my comments would
more frequently draw "Yeah, that's it. Fuckin' hey!" The sessions
would be enlivened by the excitement of shared experience, as my
clients felt understood and I revisited my own issues.

Of all the issues that touched these men, those related to
women and sexuality resonated the most. These men had intense
feelings about their relationships with women—deep scars, fears,
insecurities, and bitter resentments. The changing culture of the
previous twenty years had left them confused and frustrated. In the
midst of this profusion of negative emotions, I found these men
continuing to hold many of the same expectations and desires for
women, including the Centerfold Syndrome. The only difference
now seemed to be that whereas once only extremely attractive
women seemed to have power over men, now all women seemed
to have more power than ever.

This perception of women's dramatically increasing power, and
men's concomitant feelings of decreasing personal power, seemed
to leave these men deeply threatened and bitter. The most graphic
expressions of rage against these new circumstances were frequently
couched in physical terms—reactions against a woman's body as
stimulator of greatest temptations, provider of greatest pleasure, and
cause of greatest sufferings.

REFLECTIONS ON A LIFE WITH
THE CENTERFOLD SYNDROME

Considering my own life experiences, I'm convinced that by failing to pay greater attention to the various strains of the Centerfold
Syndrome, we're all missing something very important. We can't
hope to understand how men deal with women without under-

standing this widespread phenomenon. It's been a major mistake to dismiss men's reactions to women's bodies as a biological inevitability that has annoying but marginally relevant implications. By studying men's feelings about women's bodies we can gain unique access to men's deepest feelings about manhood and about the myriad of complex feelings they hold toward women.

While men have been encouraged to glorify the objective physical aspects of women, in many ways women have been encouraged to believe that men are naturally preoccupied with looking at them, fixated on their body parts, and forever dependent on the comfort of a women's nurturance. Many have come to believe that successful relations with men depend on acceptance of these "realities," and have become victims of immense psychic and physical damage. At the same time, we men have been encouraged to glorify the objective physical aspects of women. We have been taught to compete with each other, with women's bodies as prizes. We have been led to believe that manhood must be validated through performance, often through sexual conquest of women. We have been allowed to seek comfort and nurturance from women's bodies, but conditioned to restrict our awareness to only our sexual needs, and strongly forbidden to seek physical comfort from men. In these multiple ways, we men have also been victimized by the tenets of the Centerfold Syndrome. Women and men must both understand this syndrome to have mature relationships. Yet, understanding is not enough. We must also recognize that contemporary women and men are continually provided with erroneous ideas about male sexuality. These ideas have become so interwoven with the socioeconomic underpinnings of the culture that they are omnipresent, yet subliminal and unchallenged. We must change that; we must begin to challenge the way our culture teaches us to think about women's bodies and to think about how men can become liberated from the old patterns.

In the pages that follow I will trace the evolution of my understanding of the Centerfold Syndrome, explore various explanations of its origin, and make suggestions about how the syndrome can be challenged. Ultimately, I will conclude with my vision of female-male relationships that are unencumbered by this insidious distortion of psychosexual reality.

2

THE MEN'S GROUP

Over the past twenty-five years I have had the good fortune to witness a broad cross-section of men as they have confronted revolutionary changes in their lives. American manhood is in transition, leaving most men deeply confused about what is expected of them, and in turn, leaving women confused about what they should expect from their loved ones.

Since the mid sixties the traditional "manly" roles of warrior, provider, protector, sexual initiator, and family leader have been challenged by a complicated mixture of sociocultural forces, including the women's movement, changes in the nature of work, and the increased divorce rate. All men have been affected by these sweeping changes, yet most have been unable to articulate a cogent response that captures the range of their emotional reactions.

In the public sphere, where men's voices have traditionally been dominant, male voices have been uncharacteristically muted about these matters. Women, who traditionally had to defer to men about issues of public policy, have taken the lead in addressing how gender socialization constrains private lives. For decades they have been studying the *female* experience; men are just beginning to explore the *male* experience. This new trend in men's personal exploration has been propelled to some extent by the need to formulate a complementary response to the changes in modern womanhood. Men have been slow to fill this ideological vacuum, as "men's studies" scholarship has just begun to appear. Furthermore, very few men have joined together in anything resembling the scope of the women's movement. Admittedly, there has been some response, as some men have attempted to orchestrate backlash movements against women's political gains, particularly in the areas of divorce and child custody legislation. Some men have taken to the wilderness to join with other men seeking to rediscover the "essential male spirit." A number of men have embraced the women's movement, believing that, since both women and men encounter gender-role strain, "profeminist" positions offer as much to men as they do to women.

Most men, however, have remained relatively apathetic to the abstract ideological goals of both the women's and the men's movements. By and large, the intensity of their feeling has been governed primarily by the degree to which cultural changes have had direct impact on their individual lives and relationships. Unfortunately, in situations where a woman's changes have forced a man to make changes in his own life, his response has rarely been positive, and it often has brought him into contact with mental health professionals like myself.

Social psychological research tells us that women and men commonly utilize different mechanisms for coping with extreme distress. Women, on the one hand, tend to sensitize themselves to the signals of stress, internalize it, take on excessive blame for creating it, and ultimately engage in a range of self-punitive behaviors. Men, on the other hand, are far more likely to ignore signals of stress, externalize it, blame others for its appearance, and cope through acting out or avoidant activity, such as flight, substance use, or sexual preoccupation. In the extreme, men are at risk for behaviors that have comprised the "dark side" of masculinity—violence, rape, sexual harassment, alcohol and drug abuse. Some dark-side behavior is a product of psychopathology in individual men. However, while we must acknowledge that many of the severe problems associated with traditional concepts of masculinity are the product of a few unhealthy men, we mustn't lose sight of how these behaviors are in some ways endemic to modern manhood. We must look at what these violent behaviors may tell us about the problems men are having in dealing with the gender-role strains of the twentieth century.

To accomplish this, I will share my data base—the essence of the many hours I have spent as a psychologist and group leader listening to men in distress. I believe that the message of these men will have the most resonance if I can relay it as I heard it. As much as possible I will use their actual words, without extensive censoring or paraphrasing, despite the potential offensiveness of their frequent coarse language and misogynistic attitudes. Naturally, I will alter some descriptive aspects of the men to protect their privacy. Also, since I hope to maximize the rich flavor of group interactions, I'll take license to collapse and merge some material. The stories are real, however; the group members you will hear are based on real group participants, and not a single word is fabricated.

THE MEN'S GROUP

The group of men that provides the focus for this narrative met over many months in central Texas during the early 1990s. Group membership was diverse, with four identifying themselves as white-collar workers, three as blue-collar workers, and one as a musician. Three members were unemployed, and one was medically retired. Five were white (of European heritage), one was Mexican American, and two were African American. Educational backgrounds varied from high school dropouts to master's degree graduates.

All group members were volunteers, that is, they were not legally compelled to attend. Most, however, had been subjected to some degree of pressure from someone—a physician, wife, family member, or friend. Presenting symptoms included temper problems, episodic alcohol abuse, job instability, depression, and interpersonal tension related to complaints that they were inadequate as partners or fathers. None of the men had severe psychiatric disturbance. None were physically or sexually abusive. None were actively abusing drugs or alcohol.

Although the group was not promoted as one with a specific agenda, it was conducted in a fashion that paid specific attention to men's role strain, to gender-role aspects of presenting problems, and to the various aspects of the Centerfold Syndrome.

We will join the group during one of the early sessions. Periodically, I will interrupt the group narrative to provide relevant background material, some of which came from the group participants, some of which came from subsequent collateral interviews with spouses. At times the narrative will be offensive and painful to read because of the men's coarse language and misogynistic attitudes. I considered censoring their words to make them more palatable, but chose to let them stand, since men have too often tried to hide the private thoughts and resentments that sometimes surface in all-male settings. Although this makes for disturbing reading, it conveys more accurately the fervent distress of these men.

OPENING GLIMPSES

Roughly halfway through this slow-moving and generally guarded session, a group member made a passing reference to an unhappy experience with his ex-wife. Paul, who had been sitting slumped and quiet, immediately bolted upright and loudly interjected, "Yeah, goddamned right. Women are a bunch of cunts and if it wasn't for that hairy thing between their legs, they should be shot!"

The group, initially stunned by Paul's vehement outburst, reacted in a curious fashion. Terry, sitting across from Paul, began laughing uncontrollably and said, "Right on Paul! You tell 'em. Better get those feelings out, man." Others appeared unsure of how to respond. Some picked up on Terry's lead and begin to smile, while others looked to me for some clue.

Sensing that Paul's outrageous statement had struck a respondent chord, I decided to "go with" the feeling Paul had introduced, tried to appear receptive, and asked group members to talk about their reactions to Paul's opinions. The group, feeling permission to reveal their private experiences of women and sexuality, then began a dynamic and fast-moving session.

Arthur: See, that's the problem. You marry the wrong kind of woman and you can expect nothing but heartache. Some women are just trouble.

Terry: Yeah, you gonna mess with them, you better screw them over before they do you first. Don't ever let some bitch get set up to get over on you.

George: Whoa, now wait just a minute here. Women can be plenty great . . . maybe even the best thing there is. [*Looking at Mike*] Even Mike would agree with that . . . wouldn't you, Mike?

Mike made no response except to weakly smile and nod his head.

Fred: [*Leaning protectively toward Mike*] Take it easy guys. Mike may not be interested in being some kind of whoremonger like you guys.

Chad and Terry made simultaneous sounds of protest to Fred's rebuke.

Chad: C'mon Fred, lighten up! Look, sex is by far the finest thing there is. You can have everything else . . . just give me a constant supply of great looking women.

Terry: But don't forget what I'm telling you. You guys better be careful to not let them get the upper hand or you'll know hell like you never imagined.

Paul: That's no shit. The bitches like nothin' better than to fuck with you. [*Turning to Luis*] Ain't that right, Luis?

Luis sat on the edge of his seat, looking at his hands; after a short pause, he spoke slowly.

Luis: It's not easy for me to talk about this . . . [*another pause*] because women can kill you.
Arthur: That's definitely true. But a good woman is the greatest gift a man can have. She can add meaning to his life, do things no man can ever do for you. She can keep you sane.
Luis: [*Staring straight ahead, speaking only partially to the group*] Sure, she can do that. But what if it stops? What if, for no fuckin' reason you can understand, it stops? *That* will make you crazy.

I was amazed. In the space of a very few minutes, a lethargic and emotionally disinterested group of men had become energized and animated by mention of one provocative topic: their feelings about women. I was eager to get a better feel for what seemed to be driving this intense reaction. What I would find was that as each man described his problems in relating to women, he was describing his own variant of the Centerfold Syndrome.

Terry illustrated some of the most troubling aspects of the Centerfold Syndrome. He was voyeuristic, but highly ambivalent about the women he objectified. To him, women were visually appealing but malevolent. He was very bitter about previous experiences with women and he avidly guarded against emotional attachment and vulnerability.

Chad was similarly voyeuristic, but without the tone of bitterness, fear, or danger. Though he relished opportunities to look at attractive female bodies, he sensed problems with the superficial relationships inherent in voyeurism and objectification. He seemed to want relief from his loneliness, but was unable to let go of his fixation with new and novel sexual encounters.

George, though happy with his marital relationship, was also perplexed by the complications of the Centerfold Syndrome. Despite his satisfaction with his wife, Sarah, he infuriated her with his voyeuristic habits. He considered looking and fantasizing to be harmless fun, but Sarah found those habits threatening and insulting. At times their relationship was seriously strained by these radically different perspectives; Sarah sometimes viewed George as a "crude, drooling sexual Neanderthal," and George sometimes viewed Sarah as a "petty, harping, man-hating, feminist bitch."

Fred described a history of solid relationships with women, but he also implied that voyeurism, objectification, and lust had tempted him to violate professional ethics and had had a role in his significant emotional problems.

Arthur, who had always felt the need for the attentions of young women, experienced heightened validation needs with aging and decreased status. His relationship with his wife, Faye, had been generally resilient to Arthur's "hangups," but he was devastated when Faye needed a mastectomy. Unable to cope with the traumatic change in Faye's physical being, Arthur could not provide comfort to the woman he loved at a time when she needed it most.

Luis was far less voyeuristic and objectifying than the other group members, but he also had major Centerfold Syndrome difficulties. More than any other group member, he had been able to experience emotional intimacy and vulnerability. In fact, he had learned to invest almost supernatural powers in Mary—in her touch and her physical being. However, he had been so narrow in trusting and allowing intimacy with others, he was almost totally dependent on Mary for emotional and physical reassurance. As a result, he became paralyzed with fears that another man would win Mary away from him.

Mike was the group member most disempowered and emotionally incapacitated by the Centerfold Syndrome. He was so fascinated and excited by attractive female bodies that he became awestruck when near one. When he tried to cope through pornog-

raphy and masturbation, he achieved temporary relief, but ultimately these activities reinforced his awe and addiction to objectified images of women's bodies.

Paul was the group member in most dramatic distress and the
one most at risk to harm himself or someone else. Strongly attached
to the trophyism mentality, he couldn't tolerate the thought of
another man being pleasured by Elaine's body. Though he once was
validated by Elaine's sexual response to him, he came to feel out-
done, outperformed, and emasculated. He reacted with a vengeful
rage that was barely contained.

Gary: I notice some pretty strong reactions to what Paul has had to
    say. I wonder if it might be a good idea to sort out some of these
    reactions. Can someone help me understand this better?
Terry: Yeah, sure can. Look, women are no fuckin' good—except for
    that good thing they can do. But if you give them a chance,
    they'll sure as hell use that against you.

The extreme negativity of Terry's words was striking, particularly since he didn't appear to be an especially angry or negative
guy. An African American man, nearly thirty, he appeared to be
only nineteen or twenty. He was nice looking, light-complected,
with a smooth face that he probably rarely shaved. His dark eyes
were lively and he had a disarming smile that was hard to integrate
with the harshness of his words. One was never fully sure if he was
serious or saying things partially for comical effect. I decided to
press further.

Gary: That's a pretty strong statement, Terry. Do you mean *all*
    women? Surely you must care about some of them.
Terry: None.
Gary: Never?
Terry: Not in a very long fuckin' time.
Gary: Tell us about it.

Terry: OK. Sure. Women were put on this earth to tantalize men, to make their lives miserable. They were created to be gorgeous and irresistible, with those fantastic tits and asses, looking totally incredible. But it's a fuckin' trap. Whenever they want something, or just want to control some poor bastard, they just turn on one of those "I'm horny" looks, or just flash some thigh, and a guy is totally fuckin' helpless, man.

Terry was having great trouble with his voyeurism. He was irresistibly drawn to looking at women. Feeling relatively helpless and disempowered, he has reacted angrily against these "tantalizing" and unattainable women.

Terry: The only defense is to outsmart them. Act like you're interested. Promise them anything, but keep your ace in the hole and use them for your own benefit. Pretend to care, but be cold and heartless. Once they realize you're onto them, they'll eat out of your hand. It's a power-trip game, man.

Gary: Is that how you've lived your life?

Terry: Damned straight. I've had a string of good-looking women— whores, momma's girls, even some well-preserved older broads. The trick is to tell them what they want to hear, but never let yourself believe that shit, don't take yourself seriously. Don't get me wrong. I've cared before. I nearly got fuckin' destroyed by a couple of them, but I've learned the hard way. Just get what you want . . . getting your rocks off . . . a few bucks . . . a place to shack—then get the fuck outta Dodge.

Sexualized relationships and emotional flight were Terry's idea of the best defenses against his fears of intimacy and abandonment.

Gary: Who did you care about?

Terry: That's ancient fuckin' history, man. Ain't got no relevance here.

Gary: Let's talk about it.

Terry: Nah, nothin to be gained from that.

Gary: So that's it? You're locked into that lifestyle?

Terry: Got that right. I'm in a low spot right now—no job, no place
   to stay, no bitch. But I've got my resources—I'm a real fine
   house painter and I can get work easy. Women will come. It's
   just a matter of time before I get my act back together.

Terry looked down at the floor and a brief glimpse of sadness
appeared on his face, but it quickly vanished as he smiled and
looked directly at me, almost inviting more inquiry. I found it
tempting to pursue things further with Terry, but felt that others
needed to talk.

Gary: [*Turning to Chad*] Chad, you're closest to Terry's age. How
   about you? Have you had similar experiences with women?

Chad: Well, maybe in some ways, but mostly no. Sure, I've had my
   share of women that wanted to treat me bad, but in general, I've
   got no complaints. Women are great. Sex is fantastic.

Chad, twenty-six, is another handsome young man, striking in
appearance with his "grunge-look" clothes, longish ducktailed hair-
style, and earring, much like a star of a teenage sitcom. Though a
college graduate, Chad turned down traditional employment to
play full-time in a popular rock band. He has never married, nor
had any sustained relationships. He has, however, had a steady
stream of short-term relationships with physically attractive
women, and he described himself as "a lover of women and female
beauty."

Chad: What Terry leaves out is the incredible rush you can get from
   seeing and touching the gorgeous female bodies—it's the ultimate high. Practically every night when I play I pick out the
   most absolute fox in the audience. She may be slender with
   long, tapering legs, or a braless one with great firm breasts and

nipples that show through her tight tank top. The possibilities
are endless. Maybe a great, rounded, firm ass in satin pants
whose muscular cheeks will mesmerize you as you watch her
walk or dance. In the band we refer to these young things as
"eye candy." They charge us up, rev up the music. I've always
known that the greatest thing about doing music is that I can
get all the gorgeous women I want.

For Chad, women are primarily a collection of appealing body
parts.

George: [*Sarcastically*] Seems like a goddamned Garden of Eden.
    Where do you get off thinking you got problems?
Chad: Well, actually, I'm not sure that I do. It's just that sometimes I
    get weird uneasy feelings about this whole trip. I love the sex . . .
    the incredible rush of a new and exciting body that I've never
    seen before, never touched; but I can't help but wonder if it will
    be like this forever. It can get a little depressing.
Gary: Depressing?
Chad: Yeah, I think that's what it is. Like sometimes I'll be with a
    babe that really gets me hot, but there'll be a part of me that's
    really not that up for getting naked and humping away. [*Several
    guys laughed.*] Sometimes, after the sex we talk some, but usually
    I'm either tired or depressed. Sometimes we get together a few
    more times, and this strange thing happens. When the novelty
    begins to wear off, I can get to know her more. We talk and get
    to know each other a little. Later, if we have sex it's different,
    sorta pleasant and close, but a little scary and confining.
Terry: [*Quickly interjecting*] See, that's where you've gotta be
    careful. That's when it gets dangerous and you need to hit the
    road, Jack!
Chad: Well it turns out to not be a big issue anyway, since pretty
    soon I start noticing little flaws in her body. You know, little cel-
    lulite patches, moles, that type stuff. And by this time I've

started noticing other bodies that I've just gotta have. Naturally, the one I'm with doesn't think too much of this, and I realize that I've got to make a choice. A couple of times I've tried having sex with two at once.

Disappointed by repetitive and shallow sexual encounters, Chad found himself wishing for more emotional intimacy; but before any close ties could develop, he found himself distracted by a novel objectified body. To counter routine, he experimented with offbeat sexual arrangements.

Terry: Now you're talkin'.

Chad: Well it's a nice visual treat. But, generally it's come down to making a choice—the one I'm getting to know with the body flaws or the new and unknown one. I've always gone for the new one, but lately I've been wondering if maybe that's not gonna become a problem someday. Maybe I'm gonna miss out on something.

Paul: [*With the emotional intensity he had shown earlier*] Oh, yeah, you've missed out on something all right—a razor blade enema is what you've missed out on!

Once more we were confronted with Paul's fury. Somewhat tentative and unsure, I probed for more of Paul's story.

Gary: You've said a couple of pretty strong things, Paul. Would you mind telling us more about where you're coming from?

Paul: Sure, no problem. It's no big fuckin' mystery. Women are just no-good fuckin' bitches that are good for only one thing—and even that usually ain't worth the aggravation.

In the next several minutes Paul, who was thirty-five, told about his thirteen-year marriage to Elaine, twenty-nine, mother of his three children. Paul had met Elaine when she was fifteen and a high school sophomore. He had been her first serious boyfriend and, in his own proud words, "she was a knockout and I was the only man that ever touched her."

In the early years of the marriage, Elaine had been eager to please Paul, acceding to his preferences in everything from her hair-style to her circle of friends. Though frequently turned off by his preoccupation with sex—which he wanted two to three times per day—she accepted it as a way to keep Paul happy and to stabilize their relationship.

Neither Paul nor Elaine was aware of the degree to which they were living out a common dysfunctional pattern—the trophy wife. Capturing Elaine was a major source of pride for Paul. His need to be in control and dominate the relationship required that he select a partner with less life experience who would be dependent upon him for leadership. Deeply insecure, Paul relied on his sexual access to Elaine to reassure himself of his manliness.

As frequently happens, when Elaine began to mature and became weary and resentful of Paul's demands for control, her resistance engendered greater insecurity in Paul. He in turn became needier and more controlling. Gradually, Elaine grew tired of what she called his one-track mind and his sexual crudeness. She particularly hated his habit of patting her bottom in public and his trick of approaching her from behind and unexpectedly reaching around to cup her breasts or sticking his hand down her shorts to try to enter her; but when she objected to these actions, he became sullen and accused her of sexual frigidity.

To keep the peace, she kept quiet, but became increasingly weary of him and his efforts to "spice up" their sexual relationship. She tried to go along with his insistence that she wear the "sexy" lingerie he bought for her, tried to endure the porno movies he brought home, and even consented to his taking intimate photos of her. She refused, however, to meet his pleas for anal intercourse or to allow him to use sexual gadgets he had ordered through the mail. With each new twist, Elaine became more turned off by sexual activity, while Paul became more resentful and insecure.

Paul: The last ten years of the marriage were pretty rocky. She was always jumpin' my ass about something, usually work. So I'd lose it. Instead of going off on her, I'd hit my pickup and get the hell out. Sometimes it'd be the next day before I'd cool off.

Gary: Job problems would start the arguments?

Paul: Usually. See, I'm an auto mechanic and I probably go through a dozen jobs every few years. It's not like I can't get another job. I always do. It's just that I'm not gonna take any shit from anybody. If they put me down or treat me bad, I'll tell 'em to stick it and leave. After one of these things I'd be pretty upset, and the last thing I'd need was more crap from Elaine or a bunch of whiny kids. I never got that violent, but Elaine would get all uptight and take the kids and go to her mother's place.

Gary: This went on for a long time?

Paul: Yeah, for several years. Things got worse a couple of years ago though. She decides she has to have this little job: wiping kids' asses in a day-care center. Well, this really started things downhill. Pretty soon she's getting all pumped up about herself and this chicken-shit job. She squirrels money away, and starts bigtime bitchin' about every little thing she's unhappy about. Well, I don't put up with this crap, and some holy-ass fights come up. I never hit her or anybody, but I sure destroyed some walls and furniture. This got me to thinkin' that I'd better stay to hell away from there. Plus, I was tired of listening to her bitching, so I'd disappear for a few days.

Gary: What would you do? Where would you stay?

Paul: Oh, I don't know. It would depend. Sometimes I'd hook up with some chick that would come on to me and stay with her a little. It was a nice distraction, but nothing serious—just a little recreational fucking. [*Several group members nodded approvingly.*]

More than he wanted it for "recreation," Paul desperately wanted sexual activity to validate his besieged sense of virility.

Gary: So what happened?

Paul: Well, outta the clear blue, for no good reason she goes and files for a divorce. I'm so pissed I take off. At the court she talks to the judge and gives him a line of crap about me being danger-ous, and I end up only seeing my kids with some social worker watching over me. [*Paul began to raise his voice as he appeared increasingly distressed.*] Shit! That's a bunch of bullshit! Yeah, I got pissed, but I never hit those kids or her either, and that bitch knows it! She just wants to control me any way she can.

Gary: What happened?

Paul: I said to hell with it. Never saw her or the kids. I couldn't pay the child support anyway, so what's the difference?

Gary: That was it?

Paul: No, not exactly. Look, I was real upset about this whole thing, but I eventually cooled off. I kinda figured that eventually we'd talk and work some things out. I was willing to try to work harder. But then she hits me with the real bomb. She's met this guy and they're gonna get married. Well, I couldn't take it . . . the thought of somebody else being with her, touching her. It was too much. I was the only guy who'd ever been with her. I went crazy.

Paul found it unbearable to think of Elaine having intercourse with another man. Elaine was "his." He had "won" her. If she had sex with another man it was unmistakable proof of her disloyalty and his inability to satisfy her sexually.

Paul: I drove by her house all the time, day and night. I'm not sure why I felt the need to do that. Maybe I thought I'd catch him with her and teach him a lesson about messin' with another guy's woman. One time I had a real strong urge to drive my pickup through the side of her house right into the bedroom where I thought they might be. Guess I was thinking that if I couldn't have her, nobody else would.

Gary: So this was a real tough thing for you to cope with, and maybe. . . .

Paul: [Interrupting] Goddamn right it was hard! Who does that bitch think she is? She's not happy with controlling me and royally fucking me over. Now she's wrapping her legs around Mr. Fuckin' Wonderful, Mr. Stud, Mr. Steady, Mr. Kind and Loveable. Wait till he gets tired of kissing her sweet ass and sees what he has to go through to get into her. See how he likes her constant nagging and bitching. See how he likes it when she gets tired of you and starts sharing herself with some other guy. Sure, its great when she "comes" and screams how great you are, but. . . .

Paul's voice broke, his legs trembled; he stood, paced the room, and banged his fist into the door casing. He had been devastated by this flagrant insult. Like many men, he only knew how to express his pain through rage.

Once again the group was stunned by the intense fervor of Paul's distress. No one knew what to say, though several were noticeably aroused. Feeling that Paul needed time to cool off, I decided to shift the focus and encourage others to participate.

Gary: Well, this clearly is a subject that hits close to home for many of us. What about some others? Any thoughts?

After a short period of silence, George cleared his throat and began talking.

George: Maybe I could add something here. I've been married for a while, and it certainly hasn't been a bed of roses, but at least I've had more positive experiences than Terry and Paul. Sometimes I think I'd kill to be in Chad's shoes for a while, you know getting next to all those gorgeous broads, but generally my marriage has gone pretty well.

Gary: Tell us about it.

George: Yeah, sure. Well, Sarah and I've been married since we both were kids—she was seventeen and I was twenty. We were together while I went through college. Our first child was born during her last year of nursing school. Two others have been born since. They're real good kids. After she got her degree she didn't work much, just stayed home with the kids. In her words, she didn't work "outside the home." I got a job as an engineer and designer of water treatment plants. It's been a good marriage, though it has been rocky at times, particularly over issues of who does what.

Gary: What do you mean, "who does what?"

George: Well, I guess you could say that Sarah's always been somewhat of a "feminist," an equal rights for women sort of person. She's not a bra burner, but she tends to be pretty outspoken. She's always complained that I didn't help out enough, but we eventually got most of that ironed out. Lately, though, things have a been a little more tense. With her working nearly full-time now and expecting even more from me . . . well, that's off the subject. What I was relating to was the business about looking at women, the jealousy bit. Sarah's always been a little nutty about other women, even when I first met her. For example, real early in our relationship she went ballistic one time over some real trivial deal. We were sitting at the side of the swimming pool at our racquet club, having an intense discussion about something I don't remember very well. She was making this big point about something, when this absolute knockout girl walked by in an ultra tiny bikini. Well, without even thinking I turned to watch her go by. I mean, it was no big thing, it was only a couple of seconds. Sarah went crazy—I mean, like I'd done this really horrible thing. "What in hell are you looking at? Does it occur to you that what I'm trying to say to you is a helluva lot more important than watching the butt of some young girl you've never seen before? Am I important to you, or what? Why don't you just follow her to wherever she's going, and when you've had your fill come back here. If I'm still in the mood, which I very much doubt, I may continue this conversation!" [*Several group members reacted with supportive groans.*]

Here we see a clear example of how voyeurism interfered with a relationship. George considered his visual distraction as relatively innocuous and was puzzled by Sarah's vehement reaction. Sarah was furious because George was first unable to focus on her needs, and then compounded the problem by trivializing the issue.

Arthur: Oh shit, you're in big trouble now.
George: Yeah, tell me about it. Well, at this point in a totally irrational way she jumps up and storms off. She didn't speak to me for two days. [*The group members vigorously nodded their heads.*] You know, I never did really understand what set her off.
Gary: So it was something you never were able to clear up with each other?
George: Yeah, pretty much. I kinda got the idea that she's uptight about getting older and the way her body's changing, but I'm not sure exactly what bugs her so much. All she'll say is that she doesn't see why I get so obsessed with gaping at other women.

Given George's continued fascination with voyeurism, it wasn't surprising that Sarah continued to be "uptight."

George: I now know better than to do anything except try to stare her right in the eye when she talks. Not that it's easy with some of the incredible half-naked women parading around nowadays.
Chad: Yeah, fantastic, ain't it?
George: Well, I'm not always so sure. This thing is getting pretty

touchy with us. Another part of this looking at women thing really got us into it recently related to this sexual harassment business. [*Looking at Paul*] Look, no offense Paul, but I'm not a guy that has this real negative thing about women. In fact, I'm in favor of some of these women's rights things. [*Paul groaned.*] Now wait a minute here, let me finish. Lately I've been thinking that some of this stuff has begun to get out of hand, particularly this thing about women claiming they've been harassed. It's gotten to the point where a guy can't do anything without getting charged with sexual harassment.

Paul: Harassment my ass! Don't get me started on that load of crap!

Arthur: Take it easy, brother. Let the man finish.

George: OK. Sarah and I had a major blowout about this just last week. See, at the shop we have guys who like to hang up pictures of semi-naked women. It's real innocent stuff, I mean, not the raunchy beaver-shot stuff like in *Hustler*, but bikini stuff from hot rod magazines, maybe an occasional *Playboy* centerfold, but nothing real major. Well, this secretary, Tina, who's really quite a looker herself, makes a damn federal case about one of the guys suggesting that he'd like to see her up there, that she'd make a great pinup herself. He never even touched her or really propositioned her, but here she goes and blows things way out of proportion.

Terry: That sounds right!

George: So, like an idiot I make the mistake of mentioning this whole thing to Sarah, thinking she'd understand. Wrong! Not only did she not understand, but she also starts getting all worked up, especially since I supported the guy. Then she says, "This really makes me tired. After twenty-two years of marriage, you still don't get it, do you?" I may never understand her.

While George was still confused, Sarah had become weary of trying to get him to understand her feelings. George hadn't the remotest idea that his fantasies about Tina and about centerfolds interfered with Sarah's ability to feel intimate. Sarah was deeply frustrated that he couldn't replace his sexual fixation on idealized bodies of strangers with emotional connection to her.

As George was describing his situation with Sarah, I noticed another group member—Luis—had been showing signs of increased restlessness and appeared to have some things he wanted to say. So I turned to him next.

Gary: Luis, you seem to be listening pretty attentively to what
  George has been saying. Any reactions?

Luis immediately looked at me with such intensity that I wasn't sure if it had been a good idea to address him. He then looked down and began searching for words. He clenched and unclenched his fists, nervously shuffled his feet, and rocked slightly in his chair. After an uncomfortable minute, he began.

Luis: Sometimes I don't think its possible to be with a woman. I
  mean, no matter how hard you try, they come up with some deal
  you can't make no sense of. I mean [*making a frustrated sweeping
  gesture with his hands*] it seems better sometimes to just forget the
  whole fuckin' thing. Otherwise it may just fuck you up so bad
  you can't recover from it.

Not sure how to react, I sat quietly and waited for some sign from Luis. A forty-six-year-old Mexican American, he had an imposing presence, partially because of his muscular build and obvious physical strength, partially because of his dark, penetrating eyes, and also because of his serious, almost solemn manner. Though casually dressed, he had an immaculate appearance with fresh blue jeans, white t-shirt, and shined boots. He had thick, wavy black hair that was carefully combed. A small tattoo drew attention to his well-developed biceps and forearms.

After several moments of tense silence, Luis continued with his story, especially emphasizing his fears about his unstable relationship with Mary, his common-law wife. He was a seasonally employed carpenter, and he had become intensely insecure about his marital relationship. He and Mary had begun living together fifteen years earlier, several years after the dissolution of Luis's first marriage. Similar to Paul, he had "gone berserk" after the breakup of that relationship, drinking too much, taking traveling construction jobs that caused him to lose all contact with his two children. When he met Mary, a divorced mother of three, Luis realized a desperate need for companionship, as well as a desire to raise children in atonement for his past mistakes. Mary had been a "godsend" to him. She was warm and caring, apparently able to understand his every thought and emotion. Most important, she seemed able to allay his most intense negative emotions, his rages, his fears, and his anxieties. Often, when coming home overwhelmed with anger or frustration, Luis relied on Mary to talk with him, to comfort and reassure him. He came to see her as having near-magical powers to calm him. Her psychological massage was frequently accompanied by physical massage that led to the sexual activity Luis came to depend on as critical reassurance of his worthiness. Though he was reluctant to talk about "private matters," it was obvious that he treasured the physical relationship with Mary, as he continually made references to the capacity of a woman's body to take away a man's pain and restore his feelings of manliness.

Luis clearly illustrated the sexualized touch and intimacy aspect of the Centerfold Syndrome. He saw the world as a hostile threatening place that demanded aggressiveness, toughness, and a macho posture. Yet he hungered for an environment in which he could be nurtured, soothed, and comforted, both physically and emotionally. Mary, through touch and physical intimacy, was the only person allowed to penetrate Luis's defenses. Because Luis sexualized his intimacy needs, he became dependent on Mary's physical presence and unable to allow emotional closeness from others.

Gary: Luis, it sure seems like your relationship with Mary has been very important, but also very difficult for you.

Luis quietly nodded and fought back tears. Before speaking, he paused to gain emotional control of his voice.

Luis: It's just that it's been difficult from the start. Mary was married before, and that guy was no good; but he was the father of her children and he had a hold on her. She had this need to keep going back to him. We had lots of problems about that. I wanted to kill him. Well, we sorta got past that when this thing came up with her and her politics. She got all involved working in the community center, organizing the campaign of a La Raza city council candidate. She was hanging around at the head-quarters with all those "important" people, feeling like she was special, never at home.

Gary: That was a problem?

Luis: Of course! She'd be gone all the time. Being around these guys with their white shirts and ties. When I'd say something, she'd laugh and call me foolish. She'd joke with me, say she didn't care about anybody else, and tease me, calling me a "macho pig." She'd make me laugh, but I don't think she really understood those guys like I do.

Gary: What do you mean?

Luis: [*Smiling and looking at Terry and Chad*] You know, like these "pussy hounds."

Everyone laughed at Luis's teasing. In mock protest, Terry responded.

Terry: Come on, Luis, gives us a break, we're harmless.

Luis: [*Enjoying the more lighthearted interchange*] Sure, give you a break, huh. You're like most guys. Act real interested in what she's doing just to get into her pants.

Though not into trophyism himself, Luis was especially sensitive to the pattern in other men. Since he limited his trust to Mary and had low regard for his intimacy potential with other men, he was unusually suspicious when Mary interacted with men.

Gary: Sounds like you've hit a nerve around here. How did it go when you told Mary about your concerns?

Luis: Not so good. She got all pissed off. Said I had one thing on the brain.

Gary: So you couldn't work it out?

Luis: Not even close. She'd get all innocent and pure, pretending she didn't know what was going on. Then she'd get all pissed off, saying I couldn't control her. That would set me off and I'd tell her she could have a divorce if she wanted one so damn bad.

Once again, there seemed to be lots of potential for exploring Luis's story further, but I felt the need to keep moving and get everyone's perspective on the issue.

Gary: It certainly sounds like there's plenty of tension in the relationships with women. Many of you seem to find women both important yet pretty hard to understand.

Arthur: Doc, you're not supposed to understand. Women are different creatures. God made them different and we aren't ever going to understand their mysterious ways. The trick is to find one that treats you right and then keep her in her place. If you ever let them get the idea that you need them, or that they can get away with telling you what to do, they'll be nuthin' but trouble.

Gary: Say more.

Arthur: Well, now take my situation with Faye. Faye's a good woman—civil, a respectable Christian, a good mother, and she takes care of herself. Years ago she started getting the idea that she could run the show—upset the balance of things. Well, I straightened her out right away. There's only one master in a household and without that leadership there's hell to pay. I firmly explained the facts of life to her: as long as I was putting the dinner on the table, there would be male leadership in our house.

The group listened attentively as Arthur spoke. His reaction seemed common for him. He was an imposing figure: an African American man of 250 to 270 pounds, sixty-two years old, with distinguished, graying hair, a deep voice, and slow yet articulate speech. Married to Faye for more than forty years, with four daughters and one son, he was a highly respected leader of his community and a deacon in his church. He had worked for more than thirty-five years teaching high school industrial arts, before diabetes and heart disease forced him into medical retirement. Arthur's failing health had become a central issue in his life. Losing his work was difficult enough, but his doctors also had suggested that he give up all drinking and cigar smoking, an impossibility if he were to continue frequenting his favorite retirement hangout—the local men's club, where African American men gathered to play cards, "shoot the bull," and swap stories.

Initially, he had tried to comply, and under heavy pressure from Faye, his mother, and his daughters, he had given up his weekend card games and domino tournaments. The result had been nearly catastrophic, as he quickly became depressed, quarrelsome, and argumentative with his family, except with Arthur, Jr., who took his father's side against the "carping women."

Gary: So you see the issue between you and Faye as one of control?
Arthur: Now you're getting the picture, Doc. You see, these women are trying to take advantage of an opportunity—they're simply trying to domesticate the old lion. Sure, they say they're just trying to look out for my health, but you can be sure that this is part of women's ways of trying to do what they always do—keep a man from doing what he needs to do.
Gary: What he needs to do?

Arthur: Right. Do what God intended: take charge of the family and run the show. Well, I went along with their female power thing for about two weeks before I finally got fed up and told them to leave me alone. I marched out of the house and went straight back to the club. Needless to say, they didn't like this much and it got to be World War III around there. They seemed determined to control me, saying my life was at stake. Hell, I'd rather die proud than be a sissy-man under some woman's thumb.

Gary: I'm not sure I understand how going along with their concern that you follow the doctor's orders makes you a sissy-man.

Arthur: Doc, you sure can be dumb. The problem is that if I start letting them take over, we would have a revolution, an overthrow of the government. I guess we need to bring in another part of the problem here. Faye has never liked me going around the club, but has never really said why. To be honest, I think that one big reason is that she knows there are younger women that hang around there. I don't think she likes me lookin' and flirtin'. Well, that's a damn shame, 'cause as far as looking at pretty young women, that will never be a negotiable issue. Lookin' at pretty young things is what keeps me goin', keeps my motor runnin'. The day I can't tease and nuzzle up next to some sweet little lady, you can go ahead and order my casket. Ol' Arthur's got bunches of young women who play up to him, smile, flirt, and want to rub up against a somebody. [*As he reflected, he grinned and stroked his substantial girth.*] Sure, everybody knows the ol' lion is harmless. He won't do nuthin'. Just playin'. Just chargin' up the batteries. In fact, I know that lately that's gotten to be the biggest part of it. Faye's just jealous and wants to keep me away from other women.

Though not sexually active at that point in his life, Arthur continued to objectify women and seek regular validation of his sex appeal and his masculinity.

Gary: Lately?

Arthur: Yeah, Faye's had some health problems that haven't made
   things any better.
Gary: Do you want to say more about that?
Arthur: Guess I can. Last year Faye had a little cancer thing and
   they had to cut her up some. Messed her up pretty bad.

Arthur paused, but seemed interested in talking more, so I
pressed further.

Gary: You mean it messed her up emotionally? Physically? Both?
Arthur: Both, I guess. They tore her up pretty good. Took most
   all . . . ah . . . [*motioning to the right breast area*] took nearly the
   whole thing. I'm not too sure about it, have kinda been keeping
   my distance.
Gary: How long has it been?
Arthur: Oh, I'm not sure. Maybe eight, nine months now.
Gary: You and she haven't talked about it?
Arthur: No, not really; just been leaving well enough alone. Guess
   she talks with the girls about it.
Gary: What about you? How are you dealing with it?
Arthur: Nothing in particular. I try not to think about it. [*He
   paused.*] I kinda hate thinking about her all cut up and . . .
   what's the word? Mutilated?

Here we see a dramatic example of a problem resulting from
the objectification of women. Since Arthur glorified women's bodies, and had been relatively unable to develop a deeper emotional
connection with Faye, he was devastated by the traumatic physical change in her. At another level, of course, Arthur was confronted with the possible complete loss of his wife, a terrifying
prospect that raised the larger issue of his emotional dependence
upon her.

The group was stone silent. No one moved. No one seemed to
have any idea how to react. Normally, I would have let the silence

run its course, helping Arthur to explore his emotions and the group members to get a better feel for their strong reactions to what Arthur had introduced. However, since this was early in the group's development, I decided that for that moment I'd continue moving along to get all members to "weigh in" on the topic of relationships with women.

Gary: Arthur, I think you've introduced some things that all of us have some strong feelings about. Do you want to get into that a little more now, or would you rather we get Fred and Mike's ideas about this topic of relating with women?

Arthur: [*Seeming to welcome the chance to shift focus*] Yeah, Doc, let's let these other boys say something [*looking across the room at Fred*]. Now, take Fred here. He's a college professor. I bet he's got lots of interesting ideas about this.

Gary: What about you, Fred? You're near Arthur's age. You've been pretty quiet. How about giving us your perspective on all this?

Fred smiled, but said nothing at first, remaining characteristically quiet and pensive. A trim, intelligent-appearing man of fifty-nine, he looked more like a man in his late forties. Fred stood out from the others with his genteel, upper-middle-class, professorial appearance. Clearly one of the more thoughtful and psychologically minded members of the group, Fred had remained quiet, observing more than participating. Though not a leader, his presence in the first few sessions had been appreciated, since he was almost always one of the first to recognize discomfort or distress in any of the group members (or group leader) and was eager to provide emotional support or empathic words.

Over his lifetime, Fred had struggled with bouts of major depression that had lessened somewhat in recent years. His faculty position at a local junior college had become unsettled because of the school's increasing financial hardships. The prospect of forced retirement had created existential anxiety and fear of a return of "the black hole."

Despite his eagerness to help others, Fred was doggedly resistant to revealing much about himself, skillfully parrying all curiosity by shifting focus onto others with "more pressing" issues. Though he had occasionally made references to his first marriage and alluded to pain from his estranged relationship with his three adult children, he had been unwilling to reveal much at all about his current relationship.

Before saying anything, Fred scanned the room, seeming to seek verification of the invitation to participate. Noting welcome looks, he began.

Fred: I'm mostly just listening, but if nobody else needs to say anything right now, I'll add a few things. I guess I have a different slant than most of the others. Sure, I've had relationships with women that went badly, but in general I've had very satisfying experiences. I've found the women in my life to have been sensitive, caring, and empathic. Several women have been the most influential people in my life: my younger sister, two colleague faculty members, and even my ex-wife have been significant sources of support for me through some very difficult times. When I've had my darkest and most desperate depressions, I've usually found a woman to support me. I guess this sounds dumb, but sometimes just getting a warm embrace has made a big difference. [*Luis made a distasteful facial expression and looked at Fred in a quizzical manner.*] When I was a kid, a woman teacher was very helpful after a cry-for-help suicide gesture. A woman therapist kept me sane during the divorce proceedings several years ago. I don't share the thinking that women are out to hurt or control men. In fact, I've witnessed a great deal more harm directed at women by men, than the other way around.

At this point, Paul and Terry became visibly restless. Paul scanned the other group members to assess their reactions to Fred's comments; Terry simply muttered, "Shit, where you been hanging man?" Fred, clearly sensitive about reactions to his differing views, went on.

Fred: Please don't misunderstand. I know there are plenty of harmful women and I may be unusual. Also, I can easily relate to
what George and Chad were saying about visual preoccupation.
I love watching a beautiful body. In fact, sometimes I get so distracted by a beautiful young student that I worry about being
able to maintain objectivity and professional distance. I could
probably, if I let myself, become so obsessed with sexual fantasies
that my teaching and my relationship could be jeopardized. In
the past, I've had a few lust-driven, impulsive sexual liaisons
that were extremely exciting, but by and large, were big mistakes. I've certainly paid a price for them with psychotherapy
and antidepressant medications. In fact . . .

Fred's reference to problems with "beautiful bodies" implied difficulty with voyeurism and objectification, but he was too guarded
to reveal the extent of his problems. Just as he seemed to be gathering momentum, Fred caught himself, and decided against further
revelation. Instead, he turned to Mike.

Fred: Well that's enough of me dominating the conversation. Mike,
you haven't had a chance to participate. Why don't you talk
about something?

Before letting Fred shift completely, I decided to press a little.

Gary: Fred, are you sure you don't want to say just a bit more about
those relationships?
Fred: I'm not really sure of anything. Maybe I'll let that go for now,
except to say this. Whenever I've gotten all sexually worked up
over some strange young beautiful body, I've very often found
that I've seriously damaged a very good relationship for a cheap
one-night stand that leaves me feeling very crazy and empty.

Terry: Shit, man, do me a favor. Next time you're gettin' ready to
pass up one them beautiful bodies, give me a shout. I'll gladly
take her off your hands and give her a one-night stand she won't
soon forget!

Several members laughed, including Fred.

Fred: Terry, you're hopeless! Now seriously, let's hear from Mike.
Mike, talk to us about you.

Mike, who had been looking down, studying his hands, seemed
startled by sudden attention. He glanced around the group, giving
off a "no way will I talk" look tinged with a desire to join in.

Mike: [*Hesitantly*] It's just that I really don't have much to add. I, uh,
don't really have that much . . . uh . . . what you might call . . .
uh . . . experience in this area.
Terry: Oh, now I get the picture, a rookie. A virgin.

Mike nervously shifted in his seat, and several group members
instantly swung their heads to stare disapprovingly at Terry.

Terry: Hey, back off. Don't take me wrong. It's totally fine to be
"cherry." I just don't think you need to be shy or apologetic
about it. [*He smiled engagingly at Mike.*] You don't need to
cover up anything, or beat around the bush. You are who you
are, man.

Mike seemed reassured by the group's encouragement, but nevertheless, he continued to look around before venturing further.
Hopeful that someone would take him off the spot, he waited, but
eventually gave in.

Mike: I don't really have much to add. I guess the basic thing is that
women scare me to death—especially the really beautiful ones.

I've never been much of a talker or socializer anyway, but when I get near a real sexy girl, I start shaking and feeling sick to my stomach; I can't think or talk, but I enjoy looking at her so much, like some irresistible power comes over me. [*He paused.*] I'd better not say too much. [*The group encouraged him to continue.*] Well, it's like some physical force takes over that I can't control.

Once again, we see the peculiar way that objectification and voyeurism disempower men. Unfortunately, some men, such as Terry, try to cope with the disempowerment they feel in a variety of unhealthy ways.

Mike: Like yesterday. I was in a video store checkout. A very sexy girl with nice breasts was in the line beside me. It was tough enough that she didn't have a bra on and I could see the outline of her nipples. That really shook me up. I mean, that's a tough enough place for me with all the girlie posters for the X-rated videos, but it was really tough then. I couldn't stop myself from staring at her breasts. Well, she noticed of course, and gave me this real ticked-off look and went to another checkout line. By this time . . .

Mike noticed the tension in his own voice, stopped talking, and looked down at his feet. The group members came to his aid.

George: Hey, Mike, relax. We all get like that around real sexy broads. They have a way of making you stupid.
Terry: Yeah. They enjoy that shit, too. Should have asked the big-titted bitch to share the wealth.

Mike, surprised by Terry's audacity, looked at him with a mixture of shock and admiration, as if he'd take great satisfaction in such a brazen posture, yet was resigned that this would be inconceivable for him.

At thirty-six, Mike had had virtually no intimate connections with women, no dating experience, and no romantic attachments. Though physically attractive enough, he was excessively polite and deferential. He seemed to be intensely uncomfortable in most social situations, particularly around women. He spoke in a soft voice and rarely made direct eye contact.

In high school Mike was a good student and he continued to do well in college until he lost interest. He eventually left school and took a job as a bank teller. In that setting, Mike found himself surrounded by attractive women, some of whom occasionally made social overtures to him. That aroused considerable ambivalence in him, because he was enormously attracted to them yet overwhelmed by the prospect of a relationship.

Mike's social discomfort initially prevented him from making much use of the group, but he eventually became secure enough to begin revealing some of his anxiety about women and sexuality.

Mike: I really must enjoy looking at them, since I get obsessed with it. But I really get scared when they get close and want to talk. Part of the problem is that I start mentally undressing them, imagining how they'd look posing for a magazine layout. I catch myself staring at their bodies and that gets me so excited and emotionally distracted, pretty soon I can't even function. It's a big problem; sometimes I think I'll explode if I keep getting so charged up.

George: I can relate to that feeling.

Fred: Right, unbridled lust can ruin your life if you're not careful.

Terry: That ain't no shit. You'd better get a handle on that man, or pretty soon you'll get "pussy psychosis." What you need is to get laid real regular or your damned brain will explode from the pressure.

Mike smiled weakly at Terry, then returned to studying his fingernails, intimidated by Terry's suggestions and increasingly uncomfortable with the group's attention.

DISTRESSED MEN AND
THE CENTERFOLD SYNDROME

This session, and many remarkably similar, have been played out repeatedly during the past fifteen years of my work in men's therapy groups. Over and over, I've discovered the remarkable fact that when the topic is women, women's bodies, and sexuality, men become animated, involved, and interested. Group sessions take on energy and enthusiasm as men get a rare chance to talk about an issue central to their lives, yet typically left undiscussed.

But why has there been so much silence? Partly because of the rudimentary understanding of the problems; partly because men in groups, particularly when no women are present, rarely have such deep and sustained conversations about meaningful personal issues; and partly because of powerful taboos against talking about sex.

My own professional training seemed to have programmed me to tolerate little sex talk, encouraging me instead to shift quickly into more "clinically relevant" psychological issues. So, when men began talking about their powerful and conflicted feelings about women and their bodies, I'd shift the discussion into more "meaningful" discussions about tolerance of intimacy, ambivalence about relationships, and fears of dependency. Not surprisingly, most men become much less enthusiastic when conversation is shifted from women's breasts to more abstract topics.

Somewhere along the way, however, I began experimenting with a new style—going with the discussion—letting men talk at length about how women's bodies affect them. In doing so I discovered a number of repetitive themes regarding the problems men have relating to the bodies of women. Interestingly, these were very similar to themes I had been observing and wrestling with in my own life.

In a somewhat unsettling fashion, I discovered a crucial fact: that despite professionalism, training, and commitment to the ethical guidelines of my discipline, I, like most other male therapists, had been socialized to have the same conflictual issues—including those related to women and women's bodies—that almost all men have. To some degree, most of us still have these conflicts. This is a disquieting idea, as most of us therapists would prefer to think of ourselves as largely beyond these psychologically immature ways of relating to women. In fact, many men have accomplished considerable growth in this area. However, the growth of individual men must not draw attention away from the crucial reality that the culture continues to encourage men to retain the dysfunctional patterns of relating to women's bodies that I have conceptualized as the Centerfold Syndrome. This syndrome, though not a full-blown diagnostic entity by itself, nevertheless manifests distinctive features that are ubiquitous and principal contributors to dysfunctional male-female relationships.

In this chapter I have borrowed the actual words of men in distress to illustrate the importance of the patterns that constitute the Centerfold Syndrome. Each man, in his way, was wrestling with a unique variant of this malady and was a living case study of its ramifications. Some of the men—Mike, Fred, George, Chad, and Arthur—were troubled by voyeuristic sexuality: Mike seemed to have found pornography an irresistible avenue of sexual expression; Fred and George found that voyeuristic habits greatly interfered with their capacity to have emotionally intimate and sustained monogamous relationships; and Arthur found that extreme emphasis on physical aspects of women crippled his ability to cope with tragic alterations in his partner's physical being. The trophyism aspect of the Centerfold Syndrome seemed to have played a major role in Paul's inability to cope with his divorce from Elaine; since he desperately tended to view her as his sexual property, he couldn't bear the thought of her body being possessed by another man. In less dramatic ways, both Terry and Chad also seemed wrapped up in this dehumanizing pattern of sexual competition for women's bodies.

The need for validation seemed a major issue for both Luis and Paul. Each desperately sought confirmation as sexual performers to compensate for their failures as breadwinners. Terry seemed to feel that a steady stream of sexual conquests would promote self-esteem and protect him from emotional emptiness. Luis, Terry, and Mike all had major constrictions in their capacity to allow emotional intimacy. Luis was able to express vulnerability to Mary, but became so reliant on her that he was terrified of losing her nurturance. Chad, Terry, and Mike were so afraid of emotional intimacy that they limited themselves to unidimensional relationships with women—Chad and Terry to sex-only contacts with relative strangers, and Mike to fantasies with magazines and videos.

In the chapters that follow, I will further explore the dimensions of the Centerfold Syndrome, investigate the causes, illustrate the utterly vital role it plays in men's lives, and suggest ways for men to develop more emotionally and sexually satisfying relationships with women.

3

DEBUNKING CONVENTIONAL WISDOM

It is my hope that this account of work with men will make visible that many men are deeply troubled and confused, and that their pain is rooted in their sexual confusion and manifested by the Centerfold Syndrome. The first step in overcoming the syndrome is exposing it, that is, acknowledging that it exists and is anything but a trivial little quirk in men's relationships with women; but if this is so, the next logical step is to ask, So what? Can anything be done about it? Is it just a natural part of how men are made and therefore pretty much inevitable?

Many of the group members approached the subject from that viewpoint. Arthur made a lot out of the opinion that men's sexuality is a simple result of how God made women and men; Fred thought that men evolved into their ways of relating with women; Chad seemed to feel that hormones governed his interactions with women; and George was most impressed with the role of his peer group and the laws of the sexual marketplace. These men are not scholars or scientists, of course, but their ideas are fairly good representations of the various theories held within academic and scientific communities. Let's look at the various theories.

NATURE VERSUS NURTURE

All theories about the underlying causes of men's sexual behavior can be thought of as grounded in either "nature" or "nurture." The first perspective, that nature is the source of sex-related characteristics, is consistent with the idea that almost all males across the ages are born with an essential, basic, or innate set of preferences—that men's sexuality is "hardwired." From this perspective, the male sexual nature is fundamentally different from the female sexual nature. Whatever cause is cited—evolution, biological makeup, brain structure, hormones, or God's will—the essentialist perspective holds sacred the idea that women and men are fundamentally opposite. In fact, essentialists will argue that to discount these differences is like "fooling with mother nature." To the nature advocate, the Centerfold Syndrome is inevitable—a "boys will be boys" phenomenon.

The second perspective, that nurturing is the source of sex-related characteristics, is quite different from the essentialist position in that it proposes that the culture and larger social context create, or "construct," sexuality and impose these social constructions on women and men. Within this perspective, a sharp distinction must be made between *sex*, a biological term, and *gender*, a term that incorporates the social values, roles, and expectations that women and men learn are appropriate to their sex. According to this view, biological differences are few. Sex researchers John Money and Patricia Tucker reduced them to only four: "Men impregnate; only a woman can lactate, gestate, and menstruate." To the advocates of this theory, the Centerfold Syndrome is a product of the times and of our social context; and just as times and context change, so can the hallmarks of men's sexuality.

The second position is the one with the greatest appeal for me, not only because it is the one that offers the greatest hope for change, but because, as I will demonstrate, it also makes the most sense. Before proceeding, however, I need to clarify an important point about the nature/nurture argument.

Although it is common to think of the issue in absolute or dichotomous terms, all but the most radical theorists concede that both nature and nurture shape human behavior. Most nature advocates acknowledge that culture influences the manner in which basic instincts are manifested, while nurture advocates acknowledge the role of nature in that culture is constrained by basic physiology. Nurture advocates are just a lot more impressed with the abundantly creative ways in which men and women, whatever their physical makeup, adapt to new times and new situations.

GOD MADE US THIS WAY

Some people believe that men act the way they do because of a creator's grand design.

Conventional Wisdom

Arthur, for example, like many other people, has relied on his religious beliefs to provide answers to a range of questions, including those about how women and men should relate with one another. Theologian Paul Tillich noted that "religion expresses the ideals, hopes, and needs of humankind and provides answers to questions of ultimate concern." For many religious persons, the most fundamental challenge is that of determining God's will and ultimate plan.

What does the religious perspective have to say about the causes of the Centerfold Syndrome? There is not, of course, only one religious perspective, but there are plenty of consistencies in how all traditional religions have viewed women, men, and the expected relationship between them. Arthur captured much of the sentiment that prevails in these religious beliefs when, in a group session, he alluded to the belief that God had made men "human" and susceptible to Satan's influence in the form of licentious women. Western Christianity teaches that God, having already created Adam, then created Eve to provide Adam with human companionship; but Eve brought him much more, as her inability to resist the forbidden fruit created tragic consequences. Eventually, she seduced Adam to defy God's wishes by joining her in sin, by tasting the apple that was "tempting to the eye and tempting to contemplate." In this creation story, Christian tradition has placed the greatest blame on women for the loss of divine grace and has been kinder to Adam, who just followed his male instincts.

Religious scholars have discovered similar creation stories in Judaism and Islamic cultures. In these stories as well, women's curiosity and gullibility, coupled with their irresistible sexual allure, create infinite problems for humankind.

Even the most cursory review of religious writings yields a fairly discouraging picture of the mutability of the Centerfold Syndrome. Most of these writings posit basic female and male natures—a world rigidly divided along sex lines. Women are thought to be inherently sexual, passionate, and alluring to men, who staunchly fight to resist temptations of the flesh. Women are physically appealing; men desire them. To some highly religious persons, these positions are basic facts, not open to discussion or dispute. Presentation of alternative perspectives on male sexuality is pointless. To these individuals the Centerfold Syndrome is inevitable; women's bodies will always be lavishly tempting to men, and men will always be prone to objectify the flesh, compete for women's sexual favors, depend on women for validation, and fear emotional intimacy.

But Did God Create Men to Have the Centerfold Syndrome?

Although the religious position emphasizes humankind's unchanging nature, many Christian and Jewish leaders are not completely comfortable with strictly literal interpretations of the book of Genesis or other biblical passages. Few of these leaders teach believers that they must blindly accept that the world was actually created in seven twenty-four-hour days, that Noah built an ark capable of containing all the living creatures of the earth, or that Jonah spent several days in the stomach of a whale. Most Christians don't feel they must rigidly obey all biblical injunctions—for example, that one should pluck out the eye of an offender, that civilization should leave punishment to God, that women should be considered property, that people should never masturbate, that no work or commerce should ever be conducted on the Sabbath, and that married persons should remain united "until death do us part." In short, most religious persons recognize their religious texts as limited, dated manuscripts, incapable of serving as technical rule books for every life problem for all time.

Because of this adaptability, this willingness to avoid narrow and dogmatic interpretations of religious texts, many religions have remained relevant and meaningful for great numbers of people living in times profoundly different than those encountered by, for example, a small group of Middle Eastern men many centuries ago. Many devout Christians, when presented with scientific evidence contradicting literal interpretation of the creation story found in Genesis, opt to accept a more figurative interpretation. They don't stridently take up the banner, but instead struggle to find a workable compromise between Christianity and scientific evolution.

Women have had a special stake in the need to embrace nonliteral or nondogmatic interpretations of religious texts, since most of these texts are highly demeaning to women and prescriptive of inferior social status. As women have demanded social and political equality, they have had to confront religious doctrines opposed to these objectives. Though some women have given up on organized religion, others have worked to find a way to bridge the chasm between feminism and traditional religions' expectations of women. In 1895, Elizabeth Cady Stanton wrote The Women's Bible, an attempt to reinterpret Biblical teachings in a fashion more friendly to women. Other feminists have been more vigorous in their challenge to traditional religion and to the validity of religious texts such as the Christian Bible, the Koran, and the Talmud, which were authored exclusively by patriarchal men. Theologian Rosemary Radford Reuther, author of *Womanguides*, has spoken out against such "fossilized religious authority" that closes the book on divine revelation and the telling of religious stories. She has noted, in contrast, that Jesus himself spoke in favor of a growing and progressive religion when he criticized the narrow dogmatism of the Pharisees. As noted earlier, those people who believe that God has spoken and that his words must be interpreted to the letter interpret their scriptures as saying that the Centerfold Syndrome is inevitable. Christians of this persuasion, for instance, will always see women as flawed by the original sin of Eve; they will see men as always struggling against the carnal lust engendered by women. Such people will have no use for this book.

A great majority of religious persons, however, are struggling to bring their religious views more in line with contemporary realities. Just as many Christians no longer expect women to serve and obey their husbands as commanded by the apostle Paul, they will likewise reject outdated ideas about male and female sexuality. For these persons, the Centerfold Syndrome is no more inevitable than the need for women to be men's property. These people are not antireligion; rather, they are deeply committed to a growing and evolving religion that allows men and women to have equal standing in the eyes of God.

IT'S BIOLOGY

In the twentieth century we have come to expect a great deal from science, and in many ways, science has delivered. We've witnessed phenomenal advances in the understanding of the inner workings of the human body, advances that have provided prevention and cure of some of our most dreaded physical diseases. Scientists have learned enough about genetic building blocks to prevent many genetic anomalies, and if they choose, and society allows, to engineer the characteristics of future generations. Endocrinology has yielded greater understanding of the critical regulatory role of hormones and allowed us to ease hormonal irregularities. Most recently, we've seen astonishing growth in the neurosciences and have been promised new technologies to improve the functioning of the human brain.

In the face of modern science's astonishing progress in unraveling the mysterious workings of our physical selves, it shouldn't be surprising that many scientists are now being asked to apply their new knowledge and techniques to some of humankind's most vexing interpersonal and social problems. The rationale seems to be something like this: If we learn everything that can be known about how humans are structured and about their inner physical processes, can we not then understand basic human nature? Won't we then know what people need and be able to predict how they will interact? Could we learn enough about human physiology and neuroanatomy to know how human patterns like the Centerfold Syndrome are developed? Could we use this knowledge to change such patterns (if we so desired)?

Conventional Wisdom

It appears to me that a great deal *has* been learned about the physiological underpinnings of sexuality. Scientists have developed an impressive amount of information about the genetic development of males and females. They have shown us that males and females are genetically identical in twenty-two of their twenty-three chromosomal pairs, with only the twenty-third determining the individual's sex; that human embryos are structurally identical until late in the second month of gestation; that certain characteristics of the male chromosomal pair make males more subject to genetic defects like color blindness and hemophilia; and finally, that in the third month of gestation, the human embryo begins to be bombarded with hormonal substances that will determine its sexual development and structure for the rest of its life.

These hormones play an enormous role in prenatal development. The male androgen, testosterone, for example, "masculinizes" the previously undifferentiated embryo. For some scientists, the story of testosterone is just beginning to be told; they see testosterone as the key to understanding how the male embryo develops into a man and to understanding how this man behaves throughout his life. Some scientists have become so impressed with the role of this hormone that they consider most behavioral excesses of masculinity (aggression, substance abuse, promiscuity) to be the outgrowth of what has been jokingly called "testosterone poisoning."

It should be noted that there is a well-established tradition of zealous theorizing about the role of hormones. Women have long been viewed as overly emotional and irrational as a product of "raging hormones." At one time or another, women's hormones have been blamed for everything from midlife psychosis to premenstrual homicides.

What is the relationship between testosterone and men's sexual behavior—the Centerfold Syndrome in particular? There seems to be general public acceptance that there has to be some close connection between testosterone and sexual interest. After all, look at the way young boys change when they experience the first hormonal rushes during puberty. Somewhere between ages eleven and thirteen, boys experience simultaneously a tenfold increase in testosterone and the appearance of secondary sex characteristics, and lo and behold, become very interested in sex. Such an impressive set of contiguous events makes it hard to ignore the connection between testosterone and sexual interest.

Furthermore, it is common knowledge that the testes are the site of testosterone production and that a man's sex drive can be altered through chemical or surgical castration. Abundant documentation exists of the practice in various cultures and historical periods of castrating men so that they could watch asexually over their female charges (these men were called eunuchs by the

Greeks), or because their sexual behavior had been judged by civil or religious authorities to be aberrant or perverted. More recently, the synthetic drug Depo-Provera has been utilized as a chemical castrator of sex offenders, because it usually reduces their sexual motivation. Testosterone replacement therapy has also been given, with some success, to help men overcome an inordinately low sex drive.

Another line of research within the scientific community that has been lending support to the testosterone = sexuality equation is experimentation with nonhuman mammals, usually rats and rhesus monkeys, that has demonstrated that when these animals are injected with testosterone, they become markedly more interested in establishing social dominance, probably because they want access to ovulating females. Finally, it should be mentioned that some theorizing has been done about testosterone's role as a possible suppressor of nurturing behavior. Some researchers have claimed that women with abnormally high testosterone levels were found to be less nurturing than women with normal levels. This research hasn't been replicated with men, but it nevertheless has provided some ammunition for the argument that testosterone not only makes people more aggressive and sexually interested, but may also interfere with the motivation to nurture others.

But Do Hormones Cause the Centerfold Syndrome?

These arguments seem to make a fairly impressive case. Maybe the bulk of men's sexual behavior is the result of hormones talking. Maybe hormones can even be held accountable for the Centerfold Syndrome. Since most of us prefer to keep things as simple as possible, and heaven knows that matters between women and men are plenty complicated already, it's tempting to jump on a simple-sounding explanation. That would be an unfortunate mistake, however, because when we look at the issue more carefully, we find that, as usual, the simple explanation just doesn't hold up.

First, we can't make the mistake of equating simple sexual interest or arousal with a complex psychological entity like the Centerfold Syndrome. The former is essentially a physiological state, the latter is a rich amalgamation of physical, sociocultural, psychological, and spiritual variables. Sexual arousal differs qualitatively from the Centerfold Syndrome in the same way that the physiological stirrings of hunger differ from the complex of one's entire history of dining experiences. Of course, hunger makes a man want to eat, but we can't begin to understand his dining preferences until we learn about his dining history, including the role of food in his family and neighborhood, his learning experiences in dining situations, and what he takes to be his role in the dining situation.

Consequently, the connection between testosterone and the symptoms of the Centerfold Syndrome appears quite ephemeral. Women have testosterone, and though it can be shown that their sexual interest increases with an increase in testosterone, they never really adopt Centerfold Syndrome behaviors. Sure, they'll sometimes go to male stripper bars, an activity that has become available in the last couple of decades. Sure, they'll laugh at Pepsi commercials of women ogling "hunks." But I'm not impressed. Women will exercise their right to "turn the tables" on men, but the Centerfold Syndrome remains rare among women.

There's also a poor correlation between testosterone levels and Centerfold Syndrome behaviors. Men's testosterone levels fluctuate markedly over the course of a day or month, yet a man's head can be turned by a physically attractive woman regardless of the time of day. Men experience substantive declines in testosterone levels as they age (the levels peak in late adolescence), but many older men objectify, look at, and compete for attractive women as much as, or even more than, they ever did.

Some developmental researchers are even questioning the commonly accepted assumption that a sudden and dramatic sexual mania occurs at puberty. They have been finding that, contrary to

Freudian ideas about sexual latency, boys actually engage in substantial amounts of psychosexual play long before the hormonal
storms of puberty. Because boys are far more likely than girls to
engage in this "latency age" psychosexual play, developmentalists
are more convinced than ever that sexual play is a learned and imi-
tative behavior.

The final and in some ways most telling argument against
acceptance of hormonal explanations of the Centerfold Syndrome is that the studies that make connections between testosterone and sexual behavior are neither very well constructed nor
very consistent in their findings. Ann Fausto-Sterling, a developmental geneticist at Brown University, has been one of the
powerful critics of simple biological explanations of human
behavior. In *Myths of Gender*, she has called on her rare facility
with both biology and politics to pose tough questions that throw
monkey wrenches into the works of gender essentialists. After
carefully reviewing a few studies on the effects of male hormones
on "the human condition," she concludes that "not a single one
of these studies is unequivocal. Several contradict each other,
while a number of uncontrolled variables make others impossible to interpret." Fausto-Sterling labels claims of "clear-cut" evidence of the effects of male hormones "little more than flights
of fancy." In this regard, she is in line with a great many biologists
who have stated emphatically that while there is a complex relationship between testosterone and sexual interest in women, in
normal men there are no consistent correlations between levels
of sexual interest and testosterone levels (Bancroft, 1987,
p. 413).

IT'S THE HARDWIRING

In this high-tech computer age, it's not surprising that many people think of behavior patterns as a product of the brain's programming.

Conventional Wisdom

The latest rage among nature advocates is the idea that there are fundamental differences between men's and women's brains—that there is a "male" brain and a "female" brain. In a number of research labs around the country, to the accompaniment of extensive media coverage, brain researchers have begun to claim to have discovered substantive differences in how men's and women's brains are structured and in how they process information.

There are many aspects to this research, and a wider range of sex differences has been hypothesized than can be discussed here, so I will stick to those claims that can be applied to suggest that there are indeed hardwiring differences that may cause the Centerfold Syndrome. To grossly simplify, claims have been made about a number of structural differences: that men have larger medial preoptic areas, accounting for their greater reliance on visual stimulation; and that in men the amygdala is more developed, contributing to their greater emotional reactivity and more intense sexual reactivity. Women's brains have greater perceptual sensitivity, giving them advantages in interpersonal situations. Women have larger splenium and better development in the corpus callosum, making them better at cross talk between cerebral hemispheres and better able to integrate verbal ability and emotions—that is, to talk about their feelings. Men have more "specialized" brains, making them better at spatial relations tasks and more interested in "objects." Women have more "diffuse" brain organization, making them more intuitive and more "people oriented." Nature-oriented theorists claim that because of these structural differences in male brains, men are more likely to be visually oriented and nonrelational in their sexuality, to consider women as sex objects, to have difficulty with emotions and intimacy, and to be competitive and aggressive.

Does Hardwiring Cause the Centerfold Syndrome?

These ideas seem consistent with contemporary attitudes toward the limitless capabilities of science. It is believed that at last, ultra-

sophisticated modern neuroscientific equipment is ready to defin-
itively map the circuits of the ultimate computer: the human brain,
and that once scientists have sorted out how male and female
brains are wired, they will have unerring diagnostic ability, including the capacity to understand why women and men behave differently. The idea of discovering race and sex differences in brain
anatomy has actually been around since the early nineteenth century. In 1849, Samuel George Morton, a Philadelphia physician,
attempted to prove racial differences in intelligence by crudely
measuring the cranial capacities of 623 human skulls. In compar-
ing Morton's material to modern scientific methods and data, it
becomes obvious that we've come a long way. But have we come
far enough to actually say anything meaningful about neuroanatomical differences? When we consider that the ultimate
objective is to know how the brain functions, we're actually far
closer to our starting point than to our ultimate destination.

Easiest to challenge are the more extravagant claims of some
brain research. Moir and Jessel's *Brain Sex* has been particularly outrageous in claiming that research during the 1980s into brain sex
differences produced "a remarkably consistent pattern . . . one of
startling asymmetry." The authors' claims are grossly out of step
with any dispassionate analysis of accumulated evidence and seem
to be a prime example of what Le Ann Schreiber referred to as a
"many-turreted castle of speculation that we are repeatedly induced
to accept as established fact."

Of particular concern, for example, are Moir and Jessel's mis-
use of controversial research about gender differences in perceptual
skills. Whatever the minuscule basis for their assertions (the
authors did not provided citations), there certainly is no sufficient
justification for making such sweeping extrapolations. The capacities to process sound, perceive visual depth, and differentiate smells
and tastes are radically different than those processes involved in
the complex interpersonal behaviors of experiencing and express-
ing emotion, developing the capacity for empathy and compassion,
and becoming socially perceptive or intuitive. Reasonable readers

cannot help but be insulted by arguments claiming that question-able gender differences in perceptual skills constitute major hard-wiring differences that account for complex variations in men's and women's approaches to interpersonal situations.

Other critiques of brain research require referring to biological experts. Once again, Ann Fausto-Sterling has provided rich analysis of the field and generally debunked the more unfounded assertions. She refutes the claims of significant sex-based structural differences in the hypothalamus, medial preoptic area, amygdala, and sexually dimorphic nucleus. She has noted that the very few studies claiming to have uncovered differences were questionably executed, never replicated, and subject to far more within-group differences than between-group differences. The research on differences in the corpus callosum has similarly been dismissed by Fausto-Sterling. She noted that after the original corpus callosum research in 1982, sixteen attempts at corroboration have produced no replication of the first study's results.

Even the most dedicated brain researchers acknowledge that the field is very much in its infancy. Although many expect ultimately to find a neurochemical or neuroanatomical basis for sex differences, many scientists are much more cynical. At this point, only the most avid biological determinists would hold that the Centerfold Syndrome can be accounted for by structural differences in men's brains.

Finally, as neuroscientists continue their efforts at mapping the brain, we must remain cautious about how useful their ultimate findings can be. The human brain is not simply a printed circuit board that directs human interactions. Human interactions are influenced by variables at multiple levels—within the individual organism, between organisms, and within families, communities, and larger social systems. These systems are interactive in that each is influenced by and an influencer of the other systems. We must remember that the human brain is part of this interactive network; it shapes human interactions, and human interactions shape it. We cannot hope to understand fully any complex interaction patterns, such as the Centerfold Syndrome, without understanding the organization of systems much larger than the individual organism, regardless of how well we know the inner construction of that organism.

IT'S SURVIVAL OF THE FITTEST

Whereas evolution was once a hotly debated concept, it is now generally accepted by most people. There's an appealing logic to the idea that physical structures and human characteristics can be bred in and out of a species, depending on whether these structures or characteristics have survival value. Recently, several theorists have attempted to stretch evolutionary theory, which had focused on physical evolution, into a field—Sociobiology—that theorizes about the origins of complex human interactions. Originally proposed by Harvard biologist Edward O. Wilson, sociobiology has taken on an ambitious agenda, tackling a mind-boggling range of social problems: the origins of warfare and of state and class conflict; the development of systems of legal justice, kinship systems, female infanticide, and sex discrimination; and the relationship between the sexes.

Conventional Wisdom

Sociobiologists see organisms as almost always acting according to laws of survival: Which behavior patterns will perpetuate genetic copies of me? Some controversial positions have been taken based on this principle. For example, rape has been seen by some sociobiologists as adaptive since it gives inferior men the only chance they have at perpetuating their genes. Low investment in parenting is also adaptive in that it frees men to impregnate as many women as possible, and leaves the "dirty work" of childrearing to the mother.

The branch of sociobiological theory that most directly addresses questions of genetic survival—the perpetuation of one's heritage by the passing on of genetic copies of oneself in succeeding generations—is called sexual selection theory. This theory has particular relevance for the Centerfold Syndrome. The originator of the concept of sexual selection, Donald Symons, has offered explanations for a number of sex-differentiated values, attitudes, and beliefs, including many that are integral aspects of the Centerfold Syndrome—voyeurism, objectification of women's bodies, and fear of intimacy.

Sexual selection theory argues that the likelihood of genetic survival is improved for men who have a low threshold for sexual arousal, since more arousal should produce more sex and greater chance of offspring. Promiscuity is adaptive, as is the need to become aroused by the "new female with a fresh face" (Symons, 1987). According to Symon's reasoning, therefore, sexual selection perpetuates the Centerfold Syndrome, since it gives advantages to men who are voyeuristic, objectifying, and fearful of attachment and intimacy, and who are willing to compete to acquire the attentions of the "best" females.

This perspective has direct bearing on the issue of dichotomous sex differences in sexual arousal. According to this theory, men will be aroused by women who best serve their procreative needs. For this reason, they have to be especially adept at visual discrimination between women: Does this woman give the outward appearance of youth and good health—that is, does she have clear eyes and unwrinkled skin? Females, in turn, have to select the "best" males—men of high status and exceptional competitive abilities who are willing to invest their resources in a given female and her offspring. Within this perspective, a male's "mate value" is determined by physical and psychological characteristics indicating good genes and the likelihood of being a political and economic success. Supposedly, evolution has favored women who are slow to arouse sexually (because this gives them more sexual leverage), but has not especially favored women who are visually perceptive. Instead, advantages have gone to women who can easily enhance themselves as objects of men's visual interest, who are skillful at managing and manipulating men's sexual desire, and who are skillful at discriminating the nature of men's interest. Females have been selected on the basis of being able to evaluate a male's desirability on "noncosmetic" cues and to experience sexual arousal primarily from tactile stimulation (which is more subject to conscious control).

In summary, sexual selection theory obviously views the elements of the Centerfold Syndrome as a natural by-product of human evolution. To a theorist of this perspective the message is clear: our tastes, in terms of what "turns us on," whether in food or in objects of sexual desire, are a product of our adaptive history; they got us here. According to theorists like Donald Symons, men enjoy looking at naked women, they objectify women, they compete for the most desirable women, and they resist intimate connection because these behaviors are good for their genetic survival and for the survival of the species.

Does Evolution Cause the Centerfold Syndrome?

One can't help but marvel at the cleverness and creativity of sociobiology as a simple theoretical idea that has been stretched to explain virtually every sociocultural behavior one can imagine. Unfortunately, creativity and cleverness by themselves don't make for very good science. Sociobiology is not science. Its ideas cannot be tested, since evolutionary factors can never be isolated. No scientific experiment could be designed that deprives humans of social input and developmental learning opportunities; therefore, human sociobiology will always be more scientific speculation and political theory than it will be provable science. "Thus, even if one were to grant a starting premise of human essence, it remains impossible to figure out which essences are adaptations arising under the pressure of natural selection, helping to increase fitness, and which just happened along for the ride. *Human sociobiology is a theory that inherently defies proof* [emphasis hers]" (Fausto-Sterling, 1992, p. 199).

Furthermore, there is something inherently distressing about a theoretical approach that starts from the position that if a human trait or behavior pattern exists, there must be a good reason for it or it would have disappeared long ago. This perspective is quite disheartening to those who hope to change things like the Centerfold Syndrome, and it sets the stage for some pretty regressive social policy (let's learn to accept people for what they inherently are). For example, some have taken the position that violence is part of men's nature and that it is foolish to consider modifying it significantly.

A substantial problem with sociobiology is its attempts to apply observations made with animals to the behavior of humans, without recognizing the phenomenal qualitative differences in the behavioral processes they describe. Rape in mallard ducks and scorpion flies may well be an attempt of males to get something they couldn't get any other way—access to a desirable and/or fertile female. To compare this behavior with the immensely complex phenomenon of rape among humans is to insult the reader's intelligence. Whatever physiological aspects there may be to a rapist's motives, they are dwarfed by the motives related to cultural definitions of men and women, personal sense of meaning and powerlessness, rage, and the need to exercise control or revenge. Among humans, no complex interpersonal and social behavior like rape (or parenting) can be understood outside its sociocultural context.

Another problem with sociobiology is that for it to prove that there are essential male and female natures, it must point to a number of universal differences. To meet this standard, sociobiologists point to things like sexual double standards, sexually preoccupied men, the sexual division of labor, and male competitiveness and aggression; but as Fausto-Sterling has pointed out, there is very little evidence of universal human behaviors. Those that come close to being universal are actually interpreted very differently by different cultures. For example, though almost all human societies have a division of labor by sex, few have exactly the same form. There are cultures in which women earn the bread and men care for children. In some cultures, women are the merchants and financiers. Almost all cultures have a standard of female beauty, but there are sweeping differences in what is considered beautiful. In some cultures great emphasis is put on long necks, while others value large lips. Some prefer women to be heavy, some prefer thin women.

Even if we were to identify certain near-universal human traits, we cannot know whether they survived because they enabled the "survival of the fittest," or if they are simply the product of random genetic events. We also cannot rule out another option: "Quite early in human prehistory protohumans could have *learned* [emphasis mine] certain behaviors and taught them to their offspring. If the present-day worldwide population of humans all evolved from a small progenitor stock (on this point there is some, albeit far from unanimous, agreement), then certain kinds of behavior might be universal, yet learned rather than genetically programmed" (Fausto-Sterling, 1992, p. 200).

Special mention should be made of Symon's sexual selection ideas, since they, more than any other theory, relate directly to the Centerfold Syndrome. Symons must be congratulated for his efforts to piece together a theory that attempts to make evolutionary sense of sexual behaviors, but his ideas are clearly strained. The idea that survival needs require men, and only men, to seek sexual relationships based on visual criteria makes little sense. Even if we accept his idea that women have had to choose partners who would care for them and their fertilized eggs, why wouldn't women need to be visually able to discriminate between men on the basis of health, ability to work, and emotional sincerity? Does sexual selection theory seriously contend that men's erotic response to women is based on their "healthy" appearance? Doesn't experience suggest that men's visual sexual preoccupations change radically over time and across cultures? Are we to believe that a man would always be more sexually aroused by a homely, plain, and plump, yet healthy-looking young woman than a not-particularly-healthy-looking, voluptuous stripper parading on a stage?

Finally, as noted before, there is something relatively moot about the evolutionary biology argument since the entire socio-cultural climate has undergone sweeping and radical change in the past one hundred years (a speck of time to evolutionary thinkers).

> Any mechanism—structure, function, or behavior—that is adaptive *on the average* for populations *over long time spans* . . . may become largely maladaptive when there are radical changes in environmental conditions. When we consider the profound changes in human environmental conditions within *very recent* times, it becomes entirely conceivable that some of the mechanisms which evolved over millions of years of mammalian, primate, and human evolution may now be less useful than they once were. Since cultural change has moved much more rapidly than genetic change, the *emotional response tendencies* that have been built into us through their suitability for a long succession of past environments may be less suitable for the very different *present* environment. In this sense there may be some respects in which modern man is obsolete. (Hamburg, 1968, p.100)

In brief, even if there were evidence of the evolutionary nature of the Centerfold Syndrome (and there's almost none), that still doesn't change the fact that this pattern of sexual behavior is badly out of touch with the contemporary social context, which has changed radically in just the past few decades. Many men need to be very different very quickly. Improved relations between women and men cannot await several generations for sexual selection to eliminate some of the most dysfunctional aspects of the Centerfold Syndrome. The more obsolete aspects of men's sexuality need to be thoroughly revised now.

IT'S THE FREUDIAN SEX DRIVE

Some people see sexual behavior as anchored within the deepest recesses of the psyche.

Conventional Wisdom

Sigmund Freud has taken his share of criticism over the past several decades, yet no one can deny that he has been one of the most influential theorists about human behavior and human sexuality.

Freud considered sexuality to be a deeply biological and instinctual drive that conflicted with emotional and social expectations. He theorized different courses of psychosexual development for girls and boys, particularly from the age of three, when children first become aware of their differences in external genitalia. Supposedly, boys' discovery that certain other children lack penises sets the stage for castration anxiety, and girls' discovery that they lack penises generates penis envy. The Oedipal conflict (desire for mother and fear of father) that soon appears encourages boys to identify with their fathers, resulting in full superego development in boys; and, since girls do not undergo Oedipal conflict, they only approximate superego development.

As most people know, Freud's ideas about psychosexual development have been the target of major criticism and have undergone considerable revision over the years, particularly in terms of their male-centered model of psychosexual development. Despite revisions, however, all psychodynamic models have viewed sexuality as a powerful drive or motive and have considered acquisition of mature adult sexuality to be a conflict-laden process. The Freudian model of psychosexual conflict that follows the discovery of sexual differences makes this model fairly similar to the previously discussed essentialist theories of male sexuality. It expects men to adopt an aggressive, conflicted, and phallic-centered type of sexuality, to be fearful of femininity, and to be preoccupied with establishment of a solid sense of masculine identity.

The importance of this masculine identity development has been underscored by some of those who have challenged Freudian ideas, including object relation theorists Nancy Chodorow and Carol Gilligan. To these feminist theorists, the conflicts of male psychosexual development are not created as much by biological drives as by the problems inherent in the historical division of labor in the family—who does the most intimate parenting work? Since women have almost exclusively been the primary objects of love and identification for young boys, the development of masculine identity has been thought to require a refutation and distancing from the mother. This extremely painful process was theorized to be possible only when boys were able to erect substantial emotional boundaries between themselves and their mothers and in general to downplay their need for interpersonal connectedness. A subsequent theorist, William Pollack, has suggested that this need to distance oneself from the mother produces a "traumatic disruption of the holding environment" and causes boys to become preoccupied with "defensive autonomy"—the denial of interpersonal needs or wishes for emotional intimacy.

Like other essentialist views, the psychodynamic perspective seems to suggest that there is a degree of inevitability to some aspects of the Centerfold Syndrome. In particular, this theory posits that men will have greater difficulty negotiating sexuality, particularly in the area of achieving emotional intimacy with women.

Does Freudian Sex Drive Cause the Centerfold Syndrome?

Other than suggesting that sex will be a big issue for men, psychodynamic theory doesn't predict that they will automatically develop most aspects of the Centerfold Syndrome (voyeurism, objectification of women's bodies, or trophyism). It does suggest that men will have great problems developing intimate connections with women; but even here, there are signs that this intimacy problem can be overcome.

First, the more recent object relation theories of Chodorow and Gilligan shift the blame for intimacy difficulties from innate biological drives to problems in the way the culture is structured. These theorists do not emphasize castration anxiety or Oedipal conflict; they focus instead on traditional parenting arrangements and the lack of full emotional involvement of fathers. Since fathers have not been fully available as accepting love objects and have not given sons clear, intimate models of appropriate male conduct, instead of identifying with a real person, sons identify with an abstraction—their best guesses about what the male role is supposed to be. Theoretically, greater emotional involvement of fathers would give sons a better sense of masculine identity, subsequently generating less defensive autonomy and less conflict over emotional intimacy.

Second, Joseph Pleck has recently challenged the "sex-role identity paradigm" of gender development and has suggested that it be replaced with a "gender role strain paradigm." According to Pleck, the first paradigm posits that healthy development of boys requires that they develop a basic male identity, that is, a sense of themselves as male beings. If this doesn't take place, either because of unavailable male role models or because of role traumas and failures, boys will be highly insecure in their manliness and will ultimately compensate through a variety of defensive maneuvers. Over the past several decades, many observers of the culture, including social scientists, politicians, and educators, have worried that dire consequences result from the growing lack of male role models for boys. Mytho-poetic poet Robert Bly has gone so far as to suggest that this problem may undercut the essential male spirit. To Joseph Pleck, these fears are a direct outgrowth of the gender identity paradigm. This gender identity model underlies much of the fear of boys who have few male role models and is at the heart of fears about the culture undercutting the "essential male spirit."

Pleck's alternative paradigm, the gender role strain paradigm, posits quite a different model of gender and male behavior. Rather than suggesting that boys need to develop a masculine identity, this model suggests that masculinity is a "social construction," that is, a set of socially prescribed ideas about how men (and women) are expected to behave. Critical to this paradigm is the idea that the socially constructed male role is actually quite transitory and inconsistent. What is more, it calls for men to try to follow a role prescription that not only is impossible, but often is psychologically unhealthy. The next chapter will more fully explore the implications of the social construction of masculinity. For now, it is sufficient to note that for some observers, the dangers of father absence have been exaggerated. Although it would of course be harmful for boys to experience "traumatic disruption of the holding environment," or to feel the need to develop "defensive autonomy," the social construction model does not see those problems as an unavoidable outcome of male psychosocial development.

● ● ● ●

So, is there compelling evidence that the Centerfold Syndrome is inevitable? In a word: no. Let's review the arguments.

The Centerfold Syndrome is a natural and unavoidable outgrowth of God's will if you choose to believe that. There certainly are enough religious texts supporting the idea that men are hopelessly lust-driven creatures; but there are also plenty of good reasons *not to* accept the Centerfold Syndrome as God's will. For instance, would God actually want men to objectify women and avoid intimacy? Most religious people have recognized the need to interpret religious texts in historical context, and this matter seems to warrant that approach.

Biology causes the Centerfold Syndrome in the sense that you can't have it without the basic physiological equipment; but there's no good reason to believe that men's biological makeup destines them to develop the Centerfold Syndrome instead of a more compassionate and emotionally connected sexuality. Likewise with the hardwiring argument: there are lots of interesting speculations, but nothing very convincing as yet. Even if neuroscientists do find some minor differences between the brains of men and women (essentially, minor differences are all that can be reasonably expected), the findings won't change one important fact: the brain is only one piece of a complicated dynamic network of physiological and sociocultural variables, and like the other variables, it is plastic and ever-changing to meet the overall demands of new situations. In brief, the brain can adapt.

What about evolution? As noted above, the evolutionary argument can't be *disproven*, since evolution proponents take the position that if a human characteristic is present, it must be here for a good reason; but on closer study it appears that this isn't really so. A characteristic can be present by accident, that is, it just came along for the ride. More importantly, it may be present now because it hasn't yet been selected-out. This could be true of many characteristics in times of rapid social and political upheaval. And if ever there were times of rapid social and political upheaval, we're in them now. Many male behaviors that may have been appropriate several hundred years ago are not so appropriate now. It's time for us to change as quickly as possible in some critical areas, but especially in the area of sexuality. We don't necessarily like it at first, as it may seem contrary to the habits of our forefathers, but we'll ultimately be a lot better off for it.

Finally, even the modern descendants of Freudian psychosexual theories are no longer as impressed with the motivational primacy of sexuality. Object relations theorists have suggested that the developmental challenges for boys cause them to be overly concerned with separation and autonomy, and fearful of intimacy; but even this perspective allows considerable room for change when fathers become more involved in parenting.

So, what causes the Centerfold Syndrome? Let's look further.

4

THE TRUE CAUSES OF THE CENTERFOLD SYNDROME

In the midst of a men's group session I once asked group members to envision their reactions to the traumatic loss of their penis. Simultaneously, three group members put their fingers to their heads, imitating a gun, and squeezed the imaginary triggers. All other group members nodded, concurring with that coping strategy.

For most men, sex is what life is all about; and, for most men, the dominant sexual scenario is as follows: woman turns man on; man gets excited and gets erection; man finds way to get access to the woman's body; as soon as reasonably possible, penis enters vagina (perhaps after having been stroked or kissed by the woman); the man performs; the woman reacts enthusiastically and orgasms; the man ejaculates; scene ends.

Psychologist Bernard Zilbergeld, one of the leading writers on male sexuality, has identified several important ideas that men are taught about sexuality: a man is always interested in and always ready for sex; a man always performs effectively; sex equals intercourse; touching should always lead to sex; sex is centered on a hard penis and what's done with it; good sex requires orgasm; a man should make the earth move for his partner, or at least knock her socks off.

Zilbergeld's work, particularly his 1978 book *Male Sexuality*, has added a critical new element to thinking about men and sex. Specifically, Zilbergeld has broadened the focus from narrow attention to dysfunctional men to looking at the larger issue of how *everyone* has been fed screwed-up ideas about sex. He has introduced a new idea: it's not just women who are messed up, but it's men too.

At one time, the most prominent sexual problems were thought to be an outgrowth of women's difficulty in overcoming Victorian sexual inhibitions and repressions. Sex manuals devoted most of their energy to substituting a more liberated view of sex for the guilt-ridden ones and to teaching men how to make women more sexually responsive. The massive attention to the mythical "G spot" was reflective of this simplistic approach to sexuality.

In part, the greater attention paid to women's sexual problems and the complacent acceptance of men's sexuality have been rooted in the predominant cultural view that "men are men," that is, men are by nature sexually preoccupied, penis-driven creatures, and shouldn't be expected to be much else. As I have already shown, there has been considerable support for the view of men as slaves to their testosterone and their erect penises. One theorist, in fact, has taken the extreme position that men's nature is so innately destructive and that male sexual and aggressive impulses are so tyrannical that society's survival depends on men being tamed by women. George Gilder, conservative writer and unofficial advisor to President Ronald Reagan, claimed in his book *Sexual Suicide* that "the crucial process of civilization is the subordination of male sexual impulses and psychology to the long-term horizons of female biology. . . . It is male behavior that must be changed to create a civilized order."

Since the mid sixties, however, there has been increased questioning of how men's and women's sexualities have been constructed and how they have been practiced. In many ways, this questioning has been part of a larger movement among feminist women to challenge all beliefs, practices, and institutions that perpetuate injustice to women. Among their dissatisfactions has been their perception of how patriarchal culture has handled the matter of sex: pathologizing and blaming women, normalizing and excusing men. A prominent slogan of the women's movement— "off our backs"—seems to suggest that feminists are not just unhappy with oppression, but are also interested in a new "position" in sexual interactions.

Many women have demanded greater say in social interactions and have refused to tolerate any form of power abuse by men. In particular, feminists have challenged many long-standing ideas about rape, sexual harassment, and sexual exploitation in relationships, demanding exposure of practices that have been neglected or covered up. As the women's movement has grown, and as more women's voices have been heard, shocking revelations have been made about the numbers of women who have been sexually abused in childhood, sexually coerced in dating relationships, sexually harassed in the workplace, or sexually degraded by pornography. Gradually, public awareness has heightened about the extent of these problems as accusations of sexual misconduct have been made repeatedly against prominent and successful men, such as Robert Packwood, Gary Hart, Pee Wee Herman, Mike Tyson, Clarence Thomas, O. J. Simpson, and Woody Allen. Often, efforts have been made to discount these high-profile revelations as tragic "falls from grace," in which seemingly normal men are found to have dark secrets and tragic flaws.

This explanation, which I have labeled the "aberrant male hypothesis," holds that these acts are really the work of a few "bad apples," and that most other men are qualitatively different from the miscreants. Most of us would like to believe this, since nobody wants to think of these disgraced men as being like most mainstream men; but we get uneasy when we hear about events like the Tailhook Affair, which exposed sexual harassment as widespread and to some extent institutionalized in the U.S. Navy. We become even more uneasy when we learn about the high rates of coercive sexual activities by young men on university campuses.

Repeatedly encountering such news, we make painful speculations about whether there may be serious problems in the way men learn to think about sexuality. Could there be aspects of the sexual socialization of all men that make them vulnerable to inappropriate sexual conduct toward women? Even though the great majority of men never come close to committing sexually offensive acts, they may nevertheless be susceptible to temptation. Are the "aberrant" men so different from the majority, or perhaps so constitutionally deviant, that they commit acts outside the capability of almost all other men? Or is it possible that extraordinary circumstances prompted normally socialized men to "lose it?" Could this also happen to many healthy, red-blooded, normal American men? Could there be aspects in the sexual socialization of all men that make them vulnerable to inappropriate sexual conduct toward women? Let's look more closely at the idea of a social construction of male sexuality.

THE SOCIAL CONSTRUCTION OF MALE SEXUAL BEHAVIOR

More and more sex experts are coming to believe that sexual behavior is primarily culturally determined, that is, it is a social construction. Two such experts, Jeffrey Fracher and Michael Kimmel, have summed up what has now come to be the most accepted idea of sexuality: "*That* we are sexual is determined by a biological imperative toward reproduction, but *how* we are sexual, where, when, how often, with whom, and why has to do with cultural learning and with how meaning is transmitted by a cultural setting."

When theorists say that sexuality is socially constructed, they are not saying that there are not dramatic differences between women and men in terms of sexuality. There are. Research examining how sexuality has been constructed has found that in general boys are socialized quite differently from girls. Boys are taught to make a big deal of sex, to keep it in a central place in their lives. They are taught that sex is far and away the greatest pleasure they can experience and that they should never pass up an opportunity to engage in it. They are also pressured to be sexually experienced and to expect themselves to be effective sexual performers.

Not surprisingly, these socialization messages produce major differences in how adult women and men approach sexuality. An examination of relevant research results finds that men think about sex more frequently than women; they are more likely to consider sex as a potential aspect of nearly all male-female relationships, to misinterpret friendship overtures as sexual come-ons, and to have multiple sexual partners; they spend a far greater percentage of their day engaged in visually graphic sexual fantasy, are less discriminating and quicker to become aroused and sexually interested, and are more visual in sexual orientation.

Sex Without Feeling

What do these research results tell us about the possible causes of the Centerfold Syndrome? First, they tell us that sex is crucial to a sense of manhood. Sex is presented to men as separate from intimacy and relationships, as a biological need with physical attraction as the stimulus. It is portrayed as a means of proving masculinity and improving social status among one's peer group. Young men are taught to seek sexual relationships with women even if they have no positive feelings for them, even if the women are total strangers, or even if they are aliens.

In the movie *City Slickers*, a popular film about several men seeking to restore their masculine vitality by going on a cattle drive, one man posed an "ethical" challenge to another: would he have sex with an absolutely gorgeous Martian woman if there was no possibility that his wife would learn about it? The other man framed his answer in terms of his moral commitment to his wife and the effect of the sexual liaison on their relationship. Neither man questioned the strange assumption underlying this ethical conundrum—why would a man *want* to have intimate sexual relations with someone he didn't know anything about, had nothing in common with, and would never see again? Why would either man even consider it? Because she was gorgeous. Sex with a total stranger is completely acceptable within the male sexual code. It is particularly acceptable, and maybe even a badge of honor, if the woman is big-busted, shapely, or sexually alluring.

That's not the worst of it. Many times men are encouraged not only to have sex *without* feelings, but to have sex *in spite of* feelings. Many men have had sexual relations with women they fear, dislike, disrespect, or even detest. Because of the extreme emphasis placed on sexual activity at any cost, many men find themselves seeking sex against their ethics, their judgment, their common sense. It has not been unusual for a man to pay money he cannot afford for a few seconds of dispassionate sex with a prostitute or erotic interchange with a voice on the other end of a 900 phone line. Men are taught that to obtain sex you may need to take advantage of a woman who is vulnerable through intoxication, diminished intellect, emotional crisis, or developmental immaturity. In the pursuit of sexual gratification men learn to suppress fear, guilt, good sense, and their deepest emotional needs.

We console ourselves with the idea that fortunately this disquieting picture is really applicable only to men in a state of intense biological or psychological need, that it is less of a problem when a man has a regular sexual partner. Unfortunately, this is not completely true, because of another aspect of how male sexuality has been constructed: the James Bond or Playboy concept. Men are encouraged to always desire more, and more desirable, women. Sexual conquest is a way of validating masculinity. The more desirable the prey, the greater the conquest. The more sexually attractive the woman, the greater the sexual gratification. Once again, we see the hierarchical thinking so endemic to men's view of the world—there's always a better product, faster car, bigger office, or sexier woman that you really need to have to be happy. The construction of male sexuality as acquisition and consumption rather than as intimacy and communication creates a situation in which a man finds it extremely difficult to be fully gratified in any relationship.

The Fear of Women

Simone de Beauvoir said of men's relationships with women: "Woman is at once Eve and the Virgin Mary. She is an idol, a servant, the source of life, a power of darkness; she is the elemental silence of truth, she is artifice, gossip, and falsehood; she is healing presence and sorceress; she is man's prey, his downfall, she is everything that he is not and that he longs for, his negation and his *raison d'etre*."

As could easily be seen in the account of the men's group in Chapter Two, no subject enlivens discussion and stirs feelings as much as *women*. Men are socialized to have radically conflicting images of and ideas about women. As already noted, Christian advocates of the religious perspective view this conflict as a product of Eve's original sin. Biologists and biological evolutionists see it as an unavoidable result of the competing biological and evolutionary agendas of male and female organisms. The psychosocial development theorists argue that conflictual feelings toward women are a natural outgrowth of the ways that mothers and fathers relate to children. Boys, they say, face the wretched conflict of needing to separate from their primary love object (mother) and seek a compensatory relationship with the feared and physically and emotionally distant father. According to this perspective, the most common developmental process inflicts deep emotional wounds that haunt males throughout their lives.

The social constructionist looks at men's problematic relationships with women from a very different and less predestined perspective. It doesn't deny that there are basic and essential forces shaping and to some extent constraining the life potentials of men and women. Surely there are differences resulting from the inescapable differences in reproductive capability and genitalia, from thousands of years of evolving under different survival contingencies, and from the way these factors have contributed to distinctive patterns in how boys and girls have been mothered and fathered. The social constructionist doesn't deny these realities, but says that their respective contributions are dwarfed by the extraordinary impact of social context. In regard to its influence on men's relationships with women, the prevailing social context has been remarkably consistent, and yet inconsistent, across the ages.

In her book *Psychology of Women*, Juanita Williams noted that women have most commonly been viewed as (a) *mother nature—earth mother*, whose fertility and nurturance are the source of life forces; (b) *temptress-seductress*, an irresistibly alluring figure capable of stimulating the most exquisite pleasure, yet simultaneously distracting men from their noblest missions; (c) *mystery*, an unfathomable enigma whose whims and irrational desires are impossible to decipher or satisfy; and (d) *necessary evil*, the personification of what men are not and can never be, that is, efficient homemakers, knowing attendants of children, skillful social facilitators, compassionate supporters, and tender healers.

Since the mid sixties, women's studies scholars have identified patriarchy—sociopolitical domination by men—as the most influential force in shaping the cultural roles of women. Within patriarchy, women have been viewed consistently as physically, intellectually, emotionally, and spiritually inferior to men. Sometimes, in some special ways within the overarching framework of inferiority, they have been exalted and celebrated, but primarily they have been targets of misogyny—the systematic fear and distrust of women.

I've already noted that fear of feminine influence is featured prominently in the work of psychosocial development researchers and theorists; but the concept of misogyny is much broader than this fear, conceiving of an organizing and motivating force at work in all patriarchal cultures. Examples of misogynistic sentiments abound, from the familiar "no girls allowed" clubhouses of youth, to the more ethereal musings of prominent philosophers. German philosopher Arthur Schopenhauer, for example, described women as "an intermediate stage between the child and the full-grown man . . . defective in the power of reasoning and deliberation." Similar sentiments could fill up the remaining pages of this book.

Patriarchal privilege and misogyny have, of course, been principal targets of organized women's movements for many years, but only recently have significant inroads been made. Despite major limitations in what has been accomplished, the contemporary women's movement has inspired powerful anxiety among men and male-dominated institutions. Susan Faludi, author of *Backlash*, subtitled her book "The Undeclared War on American Women." The national media claim that overwhelming Republican successes in the 1994 congressional elections represented a statement from "angry white men." When Hillary Rodham Clinton, many people's idea of a modern, successful, and assertive woman, was described as a "bitch" by the newly elected Speaker of the House of Representatives, far more outcry was heard about the style of the media coverage than about the tone of the Speaker's comments.

What's behind this upsurge in backlash anger against women and feminism? Is it simply that men want to keep women in their place and remain immune from criticism or change? Some of this is true, of course—no group is happy about criticism of its behavior or challenges to its privileges. The issue runs much deeper, however, because most contemporary men are deeply confused and fearful of the sweeping changes in intergender politics. Men are scared to death of empowered women and they deal with it in the manner most natural to them—anger. Yet because they are unclear about whom specifically to be angry at, many men simply direct their rage at women in general.

But why should women be the targets of men's resentment and frustration? Perhaps because they seem to be the ones rocking the boat—things were fine before feminists started stirring things up. Perhaps it is women's newfound power and dissatisfaction that makes men so uneasy. Some feminists ask, however, Isn't it foolish for men to be so anxious? Haven't men always enjoyed superior physical, economic, legal, and political resources? To many people, men's power is the singular key to understanding all that goes on between women and men. Radical feminists claim that male dominance accounts for a range of intergender oppressions, from rape and sexual harassment to the politics of "normal" sexual expression. In fact, to the radical feminist, the Centerfold Syndrome isn't about sex at all, but actually about power, about men's felt need to control women.

This view of the Centerfold Syndrome is very much in harmony with some feminists' analyses of pornography. Activists Susan Brownmiller, Andrea Dworkin, and Catherine MacKinnon have challenged pornography on the grounds that it dehumanizes women and promotes their oppression. According to their political analyses, men derive pleasure from viewing objectified women because it gives them a feeling of power and control over them.

Social psychological research demonstrates that in public situations men tend to stare at women while women look away. However, in one-on-one situations, women study men while men look away. Both patterns are thought to be reflective of men's superior power position. By looking at without being looked at in return, men are reinforced in the belief that they have a measure of control over women. By looking away from women in one-on-one relationships, men convey the message that the relationship is less important than other, more pressing concerns.

While much of feminist activism has been directed at X-rated pornography, some of it has taken a broader tack by challenging "beauty pornography." Naomi Wolf, author of *The Beauty Myth*, has written persuasively about how culture has forced women to base their personal worth on their ability to live up to an impossible standard of physical beauty. Wolf has argued that this beauty oppression usually occurs at historical junctures when men's social privileges are under attack by women. Voyeurism and objectification can easily be interpreted as patriarchal culture's backlash attempt to keep women in their place—the beauty parlor, tanning salon, aerobics studio, or magazine cover. Trophyism is also easily understood from this feminist political perspective, since the Centerfold Syndrome treats beautiful women as precious commodities to be acquired or traded.

Another aspect of the Centerfold Syndrome—men's fear of intimacy—at first seems to have little relevance to this feminist analysis. Looking closer, however, we can see that it actually fits fairly well. To understand the connection, we need to consider men's reluctance to be intimate not as a fear or as a skill deficit but as a semi-intentional strategy to monitor interpersonal distance. We know fairly well that in most social situations, silence is often mistaken for wisdom; emotional stoicism is often taken to represent dispassionate personal control. Ironically, even though men's preference for social distance and reluctance to engage women intimately harms them, it paradoxically enhances their appearance of social dominance.

The Powerlessness of Men

It seems to me that many valuable insights about the origins of the Centerfold Syndrome are contained in feminist political analyses; but even though they inject much-needed attention to issues of social and political power, they provide no clear rationale for men to challenge the Centerfold Syndrome. That is, if it brings so much pleasure and props up men's power base, then why on earth would men want to change it? Many radical feminists are convinced that men don't want to change. I am not.

The radical feminist analysis of pornography, and by implication of the Centerfold Syndrome, is seriously incomplete. As it should, it gives considerable attention to women's experiences of oppression and disempowerment. It points out that many men seem to be deeply invested in keeping things as they are; but it cannot capture the entire picture, since it doesn't fully account for how *men* experience intergender relationships. It does not, cannot, understand that the current situation is deeply confusing, frustrating, painful, and fearsome to many men.

Men will readily acknowledge that they have been taught that they are *supposed* to have power over women, that *somebody* is *supposed* to be in charge, and that that somebody should be the man. Most men report, however, that they actually feel more *powerless* than *powerful* in almost all spheres of their lives, and especially powerless in their relationships with women. In part, this feeling of powerlessness comes from men's tendency to relegate to women the burden of "masculinity validation." This concept, initially offered by psychologist Joseph Pleck, refers to the arrangement whereby men only feel fully masculine when *women make them feel masculine*.

A critical scene in the film *War of the Roses* reflects this pattern. During intercourse, Oliver Rose says to his future wife (who is obviously enthralled and physically appreciative of his lovemaking), "Don't ever apologize for being multiorgasmic." No fool, she brilliantly responds, "I honestly didn't know I was." Elated, and immediately indebted to her, he blubbers, "Oh, bless you! Oh, bless you!"

Sexual affirmation is vital, but it is not the only validation that men crave. Men also feel in need of validation of their worth as providers, protectors, and generally solid performers. This need for women's applause and affirmation is a critical part of a bigger picture—men's *psychological dependence* upon women. Men are highly reliant on the power of emotional expressiveness that women bring to relationships. By and large, men realize that they are poorly prepared to understand and communicate their emotional experiences. They are quick to deputize women to do that for them, to serve as socioemotional bridges between themselves and the persons they love. In the words of Colonel Bull Meechum in *The Great Santini*, "I need you to do my caring for me."

Heterosexual men are not only dependent upon what women usually bring to relationships, but they are also emotionally and physically dependent upon women performing as wives in the traditional institution of marriage. Researchers have shown clear evidence that despite popular mythology, married men on the whole are happier and healthier than unmarried men. Traditional men rely on women to create the family nest. Single men talk about living in houses, "pads," "shacks," or "cribs"; married men talk about living in "homes." In the business and political worlds, single men are seen as immature, incomplete, or untrustworthy, while married men are considered more mature because they are seen as having progressed in the normative male life cycle.

In summary, the social construction of masculinity leaves men with some very strong mandates about how they should relate with women and with sexuality. In many ways, these mandates have been kind to men, and many men think that they should continue in place. Yet, there has been an increasing sense that something isn't right. The old rules aren't working as well as they used to. When men begin to recognize the roots of these problems, they will readily join the search for new and better ways to conduct male-female relations.

HOW MEN LEARN SEXUAL BEHAVIOR

So far, I have considered several "essentialist" explanations of the Centerfold Syndrome—religious, biological, and psychodynamic. Within the social constructionist perspective, I've examined the role of male sexual socialization. This socialization perspective is nicely augmented by a close look at learning theory—the actual mechanisms by which men incorporate their sexual ideas and behaviors.

As discussed in Chapter Three, for centuries scientists have debated whether human behavior is mostly learned or mostly inherited. They've asked, How much of human behavior is genetic, hardwired, and relatively inevitable? How much is a product of learning, modeling, and socialization? To what degree is the human organism a "blank slate"? Obviously, it seems, the latter perspective offers the greatest likelihood of change and would seem to offer the most potential for growth; but this has not always been the way the matter has been viewed. In the seventeenth and eighteenth centuries, human nature was celebrated and exalted, while culture and civilizing processes were considered corruptive of the human spirit. In the words of French philosopher Jean-Jacques Rousseau, "Man is free, but everywhere he is in chains."

In the twentieth century, perhaps because of discomforts about Freudian and biological determinism, many social scientists have become uneasy about "nature," and have become more attracted to "nurture" as the determining variable. They have been slow, however, to appreciate the role of learning in male sexuality. Mid-century, Kinsey was one of the first to demonstrate that culture—as reflected by social status, educational status, and religious affiliation—markedly influences the expression of sexuality. It wasn't until the 1970s, however, that a decisive step was made in the articulation of a sociocultural position by Gagnon and Simon. Sexual beings are created, not born. We learn sex like we learn everything else. In 1977, Gagnon stated it this way: "In any given society, at any given moment, people become sexual as they become everything else. Without much reflection, they pick up directions from the social environment. They acquire and assemble meanings, skills, and values from the people around them. . . . Sexual conduct is learned in the same ways and through the same processes; it is acquired and assembled in human interaction, judged and performed in specific cultural and historical worlds."

How does a person learn to be sexual? Research on the learning of sexuality reveals several interesting issues. First, although there is now general acceptance that sexuality is learned, there is no clear consensus about the exact type of learning that occurs. There have been explanations based on habituation and sensitization, classical conditioning, and operant conditioning models, but the prevailing view is that human sexuality is so complex that simple learning models alone cannot fully account for it without incorporation of cognitive variables. That is, while the learning principles utilized in animal research are applicable, they must be supplemented by information that makes reference to how human thoughts and ideas mediate the learned connections.

Another interesting though not obviously relevant point is the finding that very little is known about sexual learning among women, since nearly all research has been conducted with male subjects. In part this may reflect the enduring pattern of women being overlooked in research; it may also reflect the tendency to discount women as sexual beings. A third possible explanation has especially intriguing implications for the present discussion. Some researchers (Salter, 1992, for example) have suggested that female sexual behavior draws less attention because the vast majority of sexual offending is done by men. On its surface, this observation seems innocuous enough; but when examined more closely, it reveals a major bias or blind spot in sexuality research about men: sexuality theory and research is dominated by preoccupation with issues of deviant and sexually underfunctioning men.

Scientists often reflect their assumptions and values through the research they pursue. For example, someone choosing to investigate the effects of maternal employment on child development (and not the effects of paternal employment) probably assumes that mothers should be primary caretakers. In the case of male sexuality, a disguised value assumption has guided the research. Only when a man cannot complete the Masters and Johnson four-stage sexual cycle (arousal, plateau, orgasm, and resolution) is the situation considered worthy of research investment. If he is able to get erections, to ejaculate, and so forth, there cannot be a problem, *unless* he chooses inappropriate targets for this activity. There has been virtually no research into matters of possible harmful effects of sexual preoccupation and sexual fixation in *normal* men, because the scientific community assumes that it's natural for men to want lots of sex, to fixate on visual sexuality, to objectify women's bodies, to rely on sex for masculinity validation, to compete for the chance to have sex with physically attractive women, and to substitute sex for emotional intimacy. The defining features of the Centerfold Syndrome have been accepted as business-as-usual for normal men.

There has been some attention to the issue of men who overvalue sex or who respond inappropriately to sexual stimuli, but this has only been considered within the framework of pathology or sexual deviance—in the study of voyeurs, rapists, child molesters, and sexual fetishists. This last group, sexual fetishists, is particularly relevant to the case of the Centerfold Syndrome and will be discussed more fully later.

The Classical Conditioning Model of Male Sexual Arousal

What turns men on? We all have a pretty good idea what that is, and sense that it hasn't changed much over the years. Lately, however, if we were to ask men this question, we would likely get a variety of lofty answers: "It turns me on to be appreciated or respected." "A woman of good character turns me on." "I enjoy a woman with a pleasant and sophisticated appearance." These responses may have a degree of truth, but they don't reflect what might be learned from simply observing what men are watching or from noting how crafty advertisers and marketers are getting men's attention.

It's an inescapable fact that most men are very excited, very turned on, by looking at women—a certain type of women, presented in a certain way, doing certain things, or giving off certain messages. Men are aroused by "sexy" women, that is, women who fit into a certain physical category—women who men describe as "buxom," "shapely," "comely," "fetching," or "alluring"; women who have "supple bodies," "full, swelling breasts," "long tapering legs," or "firm, rounded bottoms." They will be seen as even more attractive if they are "dancing," "prancing," "bouncing," "strutting," or "shaking their booty." They will be seen as even more attractive if they cultivate a "naughty," "sassy," "come-hither," "lascivious," or "risqué" manner. It won't hurt either if they dress themselves in something "skimpy," "daring," "revealing," or "dangerous."

The lists are endless. Men respond sexually to the way women look or are presented. As previously noted, some people see this as a product of men's basic nature. Others, however, posit that men *learn* to be aroused through "classical conditioning," the repeated pairing of an "unconditioned stimulus" with a "conditioned stimulus" to produce a "conditioned response." The most well-known illustration of this model has been that of Russian psychologist Ivan Pavlov. Pavlov was able to show that dogs that salivate (an unconditioned response) in the presence of food powder (an unconditioned stimulus) would also learn to salivate (a conditioned response) to a previously neutral stimulus like a bell (a conditioned stimulus) if the bell and food powder were repeatedly presented together. This classical conditioning model has usually been invoked to explain the learning of sexual arousal in men. It's a bit of a stretch, since sexual arousal is far more complicated than a simple biological response to a discrete sexual stimulus; nevertheless, the model has gained general acceptance as a crude approximation of men's learned sexual arousal. In its simplest form, the idea is that men learn to respond sexually, to generalize sexual arousal, to whatever is paired with the powerfully rewarding response of orgasm.

Thus, heterosexual men will respond to the naked bodies of women because they have been associated with sexual pleasure through intercourse or masturbation. There is some disagreement among learning theorists about whether a nude female body is an unconditioned or a conditioned stimulus, but there is no doubt that men over time develop strong positive associations to women's bodies.

Fetishism and the Centerfold Syndrome

The classical conditioning model has been called upon to explain some seemingly inexplicable behaviors among certain men—the paraphiliacs, or more specifically, the sexual fetishists. To "normal" people, sexual fetishists are pretty weird guys who get sexually aroused by such things as high-heeled shoes, lacy underpants, or other objects made out of such materials as rubber or leather; but to the professional community, fetishism is understood according to the definition provided by the Diagnostic and Statistical Manual of Mental Disorders (DSM-IV) as follows:

A. Over a period of at least six months, recurrent intense sexually arousing fantasies, sexual urges, or behaviors involving the use of nonliving objects (e.g., female undergarments).

B. The fantasies, sexual urges, or behaviors cause clinically significant distress or impairment in social, occupational, or other important areas of functioning.

C. The fetish objects are not limited to articles of female clothing used in cross-dressing (as in Transvestic Fetishism) or devices designed for the purpose of tactile genital stimulation (e.g., a vibrator). [The American Psychiatric Association, 1994, p. 526.]

The commonly accepted explanation of fetishism is that men (almost no women have this disorder) learn to associate their sexual excitement with the presence of some formerly innocuous object, such as a shoe or undergarment. Support for this has been provided by research in which male experimenters were able to condition men to become sexually aroused by black boots by pairing the boots with pictures of nude women. (It is interesting to note that they considered such pictures to be an *unconditioned* stimulus.)

So, the classical conditioning model claims that normal men learn to associate their sexual excitement with the visual images commonly available during sexual arousal—that is, naked women—which would seem to indicate that men are prone to be visually oriented. It would also seem, however, that some men become victims of a cruel accident when they become sexually conditioned to stray objects within the sexual situation (bras, panties, shoes, and so forth) and can't keep themselves from getting sexually turned on by them. Supposedly, "normal" men also generalize somewhat, but by and large, they stay focused on the true target of their desire—the body of their loved one—and never become sexual fetishists.

I think I smell a rat here. In appears to me that the great majority of men are more than a little interested in what DSM-IV refers to as "nonliving objects." Men are increasingly showing indications of sexual interest in "nonliving" objects. In a recent research study, psychologist Deborah Then found that 88 percent of Stanford MBA students "read" the Victoria's Secret lingerie catalog. *Playboy* now publishes a special lingerie edition. Some will argue, of course, that the attraction is not the lingerie but the sexy model wearing it; then why not just leave the model naked?

Further, men in huge numbers pay several dollars an issue to gawk at glossy, two-dimensional replications of naked female strangers. Are these women real living things to the men who whip through the pages? Is it possible to stare at women's breasts or other body parts and not be treating them as objects? It is no secret that a great many men "have sex" with these "impersonations" of women—that is, they use the pictures as masturbatory stimuli.

Despite the arguments of apologists and profiteers, these glossy pictures (nonliving objects) are not "sex aids." Men do *not* use them to help themselves "get into" the relationships with their loved ones, but use them *instead of* their loved ones. Some use these pictures to masturbate instead of having sex with their loved ones; some have sex with the fantasized women *during* sex with their loved ones.

A deeply disturbing picture is beginning to emerge: the difference between the sexual fetishist and the mainstream American man may not be as extreme as we have wanted to think. American boys, adolescents, and men are being taught, classically conditioned if you will, to become sexually obsessed with constant, intense, sexually arousing fantasies, and to make their sexual arousal more dependent upon use of sexualized images of nonliving objects than on real women with whom they are in relationships.

LEARNING THE CENTERFOLD SYNDROME

When men dwell on the condition of their "sex organ" they usually are aiming about two feet too far south. More than ever, sex researchers are finding that the brain is the critical sex organ—that mental activity plays the pivotal role in augmenting or inhibiting the sexual response cycle. Two such researchers, Susan Walen and David Roth, have challenged the more simplistic models of sexual learning and have provided an eight-stage model of sexuality. Their model is distinguished by its supplementation of the usual biological and behavioral components of sexual response with specific attention to the cognitive processes of "perception" and "evaluation." To Walen and Roth, perception includes the correct gathering of data and the drawing of accurate conclusions from it. Problems result from the inability to detect sexual stimuli, incorrect labeling, or misattribution. Evaluation entails rating sexual events on a continuum from bad to good.

To Walen and Roth, human sexual arousal is a complex feedback process involving continual interaction between perception,

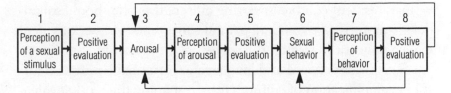

Figure 4.1. Feedback Loop of a Positive Sexual Experience.
Source: Reprinted with permission from Walen and Roth, 1987, p.341.

behavior, and evaluation. Feedback shapes each link in the sequence, functioning as both a cue and a reinforcer. As we explore this learning model (illustrated in Figure 4.1) we will see that learning the Centerfold Syndrome is facilitated by a culture whose feedback gives men easy access to cognitions that support objectification of women.

Links 1 and 2: Perception of Sexual Stimuli and Positive Evaluation

The first two steps in the model address the issue of which stimuli are perceived as sexual and which are considered nonsexual. In large part, these evaluations are thought to come about through "stimulus pairing," whereby events that have been repeatedly experienced in conjunction with sexual arousal or orgasm take on erotic meaning. Although this sounds like a simple and straightforward process, one that would generate relative uniformity among peoples, it is not. It actually is an idiosyncratic and culture-bound process that produces sizable variability in what different human cultures consider erotic or sexual.

Perhaps the best example of this variability is the way that people around the world view women's breasts. In many cultures, women's bare breasts are considered erotically insignificant; but in American culture, they are the focus of enormous erotic imagery. Imagine the reaction one would receive from suggesting to a woman resident of a breast-baring culture that she should squander six-months salary, endure painful surgery, and risk serious medical complications to alter the shape or "lift" of her breasts.

Semanticists (word and language experts) have provided further exemplification of culture's role in shaping the erotic evaluation process by demonstrating that there is a positive relationship between the richness of a culture's descriptive language for an item and the perceived importance of that item to the culture. For example, in Alaskan culture there are many words for snow, and in Arab culture there are many words for sand. Interestingly enough, in mainstream North American culture there are a great many words for female breasts, slightly fewer for the vagina, and very few for the clitoris.

Stimulus pairing is a useful but very limited concept for explaining men's perception and evaluation of erotic stimuli. There are many other sociocultural processes in place that not only enhance men's positive evaluation of naked women, but whip up worship of the female body into a frenzy. Women's bodies are the recipients of the most extensive public relations campaigns of modern times. Boys are strenuously taught to be spectators in life's parade of young women's bodies. Just like appreciative spectators at any gala production, they are encouraged to spectate as part of an exuberant audience that shares in the infectious arousal.

Boys often make their first precious glimpses of female nakedness in magazine pictures a bonding or celebratory activity, by passing the pictures around as part of a group consumption. They try to impress each other with their reactions, with their hooting, grunting, and sharing of primal excitement. Various verbal expressions are learned—"Look at those hooters!" "What a pair o' melons on that babe!" "Baby, you can pull my train anytime."—and so forth.

Within the second link of the model (positive evaluation), there is another factor that contributes to women's bodies being elevated in importance: the manipulation of the image, the art of titillation. We don't need to refer to the scientific literature to know that objects considered sexually arousing can lose their erotic charge once they become familiar. Nudists know this; people get accustomed to the presence of other naked people and the novelty wears off. This process of "habituation" invariably sets in unless something dramatic is done to enliven or maintain the erotic image. Anyone interested, therefore, in perpetuating the Center-fold Syndrome, in getting men to continue to respond sexually to unknown women, must be skilled at titillating, offering and with-drawing, teasing, and constantly finding new and different ways to package the utterly familiar. The profiteers must be able to take nearly identical raw material (women's bodies) and create such a sense of mystery, novelty, and, urgency, that millions of men will spend money to see again what they've seen thousands of times already.

It would be expected that young boys would want to see more than one naked woman, since curiosity cannot be satisfied so quickly. It should take several viewings to really get a good idea of what a naked woman looks like; but at some point, shouldn't their curiosity about generic, unfamiliar women be satisfied? Shouldn't looking repeatedly at the same general stimulus package become boring?

This could happen. Under normal circumstances the curiosity would wane and boys would become more interested in seeing "spe-cial" naked bodies—the bodies of women they know and feel emo-tionally drawn to; but those profiteers who are invested in perpetuating the Centerfold Syndrome step in to alter the process of decreasing interest in body-as-object by introducing a bounty of ways to heighten interest in body-as-object.

With skills rivaling those of the greatest sculptors or artists, beauty technicians create endless ways to reveal yet cover women's bodies. Depending on the historic or regional context, emphasis is placed on women's legs, breasts, derrières, waists, necks, ankles, or stomachs. Masterful techniques can be employed to magnify and glorify minuscule differences in the shape and contours of women's bodies, laying the groundwork for the perceptual trick of turning a living person into an object of art. Men learn to view women's bodies as beauty objects, capable of being rated like other valuable commodities—fine wines, classic automobiles, livestock, and agricultural produce. The best bodies are cherished; the worst are considered repulsive.

The first two links of this model show that the culture is doing its part to ensure that young men learn the Centerfold Syndrome. Young men's positive evaluations of women's bodies are enhanced by a culture that celebrates them and by profiteers who use women's bodies to tantalize and titillate.

Links 3 and 4: Arousal and Perception of Arousal

The next links in this sequence should be simple. A positively valued sexual stimulus has generated a physiological response of sexual arousal; next, that arousal should be perceived, and when that perception is evaluated positively, the process continues. Things don't always unfold that simply, however.

First, there is the problem of the ambiguity of the symptoms of physical arousal. Masters and Johnson have shown that the early stages of sexual arousal—increased heart rate, blood pressure, and muscle tension—are the same as those occurring under other circumstances, such as when feeling fear, physical fatigue, and anxiety. Therefore, to accurately recognize sexual arousal, the person must be sensitive to the surrounding context, to scan the environment for clues to whether or not the situation is a sexual one. If it is, the physiological state can be identified as sexual arousal, and not fear or anxiety. (Obviously, this discrimination process works best when the context is either very much a sexual one, or very much a nonsexual one; ambiguity of situation can be expected to produce problematic responses.) The process continues on track when the person evaluates the newly perceived state of sexual arousal as proper and a good idea. Unfortunately, there are a number of possible derailments of this sequence, and as usual, most sex researchers have focused exclusively on the problems of women and underfunctioning men.

The most commonly identified derailment is that which occurs when physiological arousal is present but not recognized. Often, because of poor familiarity with symptoms of sexual arousal, the symptoms are mislabeled as something else, such as anxiety or fear. This happens frequently with women for a number of reasons. One principal reason, of course, has been the traditional expectation that women should not focus too much on their physical signs of sexual arousal. Another reason may be the greater subtlety of women's vasocongestive sexual arousal, that is, genital engorgement. Additionally, it may be that women haven't had the luxury of focusing on their sexual arousal because their traditional social role has called for them to be more attentive to their partners than to themselves, either to guard against unwanted advances or to make sure that his ego is assuaged. A common problem for women then is that there may be sexual arousal, but because of their need to attend to other things (fear that he will try to go too far; concern that he is okay), they are not fully attentive to it and do not continue with the sexual process.

The situation for underfunctioning men has been thought to be somewhat different, yet similar. They have less difficulty than women in perceiving the sexual arousal, but as with women, something interferes with their ability to complete the sequence. For these men, the interfering cognitions are likely to be intense performance anxieties or memories of past failures.

Another form of derailment has been too poorly appreciated as a problem for men. As already shown, women get into difficulty when they label sexual arousal as something else (fear or concern). Conversely, many men run into difficulties because they label "something else" (fear or anxiety) as sexual arousal, or at least they may experience these emotions as heightening sexual arousal and not inhibiting it. How could this be?

First, it must be noted that research has shown that a general state of physiological arousal can increase sexual arousal in men. Second, many men learn to associate sexual encounters with a number of arousal states relatively unconnected to their feelings for their partners. Many men's first sexual encounters are in highly anxiety-provoking or dangerous circumstances. They learn to perform sexually under conditions that resemble battle more closely than they resemble a close and loving relationship. To do this, they learn to repress, or inhibit, the signals from their environment, and instead focus almost exclusively on their sexual arousal.

For many men, even dangerous and risk-laden environments can seem to tell them to go ahead sexually; consequently, men have the potential to interpret a great range of physical states as sexual ones. They have been taught to be underattentive to the emotional cues emanating from their partners. Therefore, in situations in which there is great ambiguity about whether sexuality is called for, women have tended to avoid sexuality, while men have learned to forge ahead.

How does this process contribute to the Centerfold Syndrome? It is my belief that young men learn to be sexual in environments that are not particularly conducive to intimacy and empathy. Rather than learning to "turn off" when there is no tenderness or emotional connectedness, they learn to forge ahead. The result is what psychologist Ronald Levant has called "unconnected lust" and "nonrelational sexuality," and what I call fear of intimacy.

Link 5: Evaluation of Arousal

Many women have been taught that sexual arousal isn't such a good thing, that it's improper or unladylike. Many have been taught that their vasocongestion and lubrication are embarrassing or unpleasant. Sexologists have devoted considerable attention to teaching women more "sex-positive" attitudes.

While it can be argued that many men also have been taught to be sexually guilt-ridden, men in general have been taught to be overly positive about sexual arousal. The greatest difficulty with this is that men have not been attentive to the degree to which their sexual arousal is or is not compatible with the situation. Young men have been taught to use whatever means necessary to acquire sex; too little attention has been given to helping them learn to integrate their sexual responsiveness with an empathic awareness of the emotional and physical state of their partners.

The fear of intimacy aspect of the Centerfold Syndrome is reinforced and perpetuated by this overly positive attitude toward male sexual arousal. True intimacy requires sensitivity to the partner's emotional state, one's own emotional state, and the state of the relationship. When men don't say no, when they learn to go ahead with sex just because they're aroused, they risk losing the capacity for intimate sexual connection.

Link 6: Overt Sexual Behavior

Learning occurs not only from stimulus pairing, but also from operant conditioning—behaviors followed by reinforcement are perpetuated, those not reinforced are not repeated. In the case of male sexuality, men learn those behaviors that have been rewarded. It would be ideal if men's sexual rewards came about after a sequence in which they carefully discriminated signs of sexual arousal that had been generated by a sincere desire to be intimate with their partners, and made appropriate allowances for emotional and situational warning signs. That is, it would be great if men were rewarded for being sexually discriminating in terms of partners, places, and times. Ideally, sexual encounters would only continue when they unfolded in a sensitive and compassionate manner; but when they got off track, they would be interrupted until relationship maintenance could be performed and problem spots addressed. Empathy and communication skills would be critical tools for assuring that both partners are in harmony throughout the stages of the sexual response cycle. Like so many other rewarding activities, sex would be more fun with a partner, with someone whose excitement and enjoyment would infectiously enhance one's own enjoyment. When, or whether, the partner reached orgasm would be far less important than the emotional gratification of deeply felt emotional connection and intimacy. Disconnection from the encounter would be slow and gradual, as pleasurable moments would be allowed to linger.

Sadly, most men experience sexual gratification as orgasm, after engaging in a sexual behavior sequence quite different than that just described. Men usually learn to approach sexual intercourse as a physical act that demands athletic skills, physical dexterity, and pelvic technique. They learn that sometimes, when they want to have sex with someone they don't particularly know or like, they will have to fake it. They will have to put on a mask, adopt a demeanor of sensitivity and caring, figure out the right thing to say to further the cause, and generally make an earnest effort to emulate the great lovers they've seen or heard about. Underneath this lover persona, however, there will be an intrepid adventurer, determined to complete the sexual conquest. His agenda is clear: to perform vigorously and nobly, remaining as vigilant as a master yachtsman in attending to all input necessary to guide the voyage, continually monitoring responses from his partner and always trying to look good in the eyes of his buddies (who usually are psychologically present). He performs tirelessly until reaching climax, then gets out of there as quickly as possible.

Of course, many men do not participate in sex in this way. Many do, however. More participate in this fashion than in the more compassionate and emotionally intimate fashion. It isn't easy to get men to consider changing this pattern after so many years of experiencing sexual reward following it. They have been operantly conditioned to act in keeping with the Centerfold Syndrome. They have sought out sex with women based on physical criteria and have frequently had sex regardless of the emotional connection. Even if the woman doesn't meet the minimal criteria, it's not uncommon for the man to have sex while imagining her as a much more attractive sex object he's encountered. Furthermore, emotionally intimate sex involves coming face-to-face with so many things most men aren't terribly comfortable with: vulnerability and giving up of control. You can't get rewarded for something you're too afraid to try.

Links 7 and 8: Perception of Overt Sexual Behavior and Evaluation of Overt Sexual Behavior

A man's perception of his sexual behavior can enhance his enjoyment of a sexual experience. That is, he will have a better experience when he learns to think of himself as an authentic sexual being engaging enthusiastically in a positively valued activity. However, if he's "faking it," that is, wearing a mask or playing an alien role, he cannot help but spot gaps between what he thinks he should be and what he actually experiences. In extreme cases, his sexuality will become alienated from his emotional experiences; he will become a sexual automaton.

Further, if he becomes so intent on watching himself perform that he develops the habit of dissociating from himself during sexual encounters, he will become part of the observing crowd, the male chorus he has spent his life trying to impress. If he has adopted some arbitrary performance standard (number of orgasms, minutes in the saddle, dramatic evidence of partner ecstasy) he will make sex part of his unending life's work, and rarely be satisfied. And when the sexual performance doesn't "bring the house down," he will be left feeling cheated and desperately needy of greater validation.

From the learning perspective, the heart of the matter is this: at every link of the sexual response sequence, there is some socio-cultural situation that tends to make it likely that men will learn the Centerfold Syndrome. At the level of stimulus perception, men are taught to worship women's bodies, which are artificially enhanced through visual artistry. At the level of sexual arousal, young men are pressured to blur the lines between sex-appropriate and non-sex-appropriate situations. At the level of evaluating their arousal, they're taught to be nondiscriminating, assuming that if the equipment is responding, then sex should be undertaken. At the level of overt sexual behavior, men too often are rewarded for the wrong things. Finally, at the level of perception and evaluation of their sexuality, men are encouraged to include sexual perfor-mance as a crucial measuring stick for masculinity.

What Really Causes the Centerfold Syndrome?

After all this, what's the bottom-line cause of the Centerfold Syn-drome? In Chapter Three, I outlined several perspectives that con-sider "nature" to be the principal explanation for men's sexual behavior. Each of those perspectives has its appeal and its propo-nents. In fact, some of them, such as the religious and evolution-ary perspectives, can't really be proven or disproved, making their viability more a matter of faith than of science. Other perspectives, such as the biological, neuroanatomical, and psychodynamic, pro-pose interesting but incomplete theories.

It appears to me that among the possible explanations for the Centerfold Syndrome, the sociocultural explanations are over-whelmingly most impressive. I strongly believe that the Centerfold Syndrome is a product of the way sex has been presented and taught to men. These lessons have been supported by the idea that men should keep women in their place and simultaneously estab-lish their own place in the eyes of other men by using women's bodies. They have also been perpetuated by an irresponsible system of teaching young men about sexuality. They are the tragic result of a culture that profits from manipulating images of women and grossly impairing men's capacity to develop deeply intimate relationships with women.

The bad news of my thesis is that men's sexuality has been seriously messed up. The good news is that this messed-up state of affairs is unnecessary and, as I will show, it can be changed.

5

MEN WHO MADE PROGRESS

Every man who overcomes the Centerfold Syndrome does so by his own method and according to his own timetable. Some men have revelatory experiences or confrontations that rearrange their assumptions or values, provoking dramatic changes in how they think about women and women's bodies. More commonly, however, men make small incremental shifts in circumscribed areas of their lives. Some men change quickly and readily; most, however, change reluctantly over a period of many years. Many men take steps they think are progressive, only to experience an impasse that convinces them they have regressed instead. Many men resist change altogether, lashing out at those who push them.

For many of the men introduced in Chapter Two, the group experience was a major catalyst for change. Some of them changed substantially within the group setting. Others supplemented their work with other therapies, men's group activities, or support groups. Most used our group as a launching pad for initiating changes with family members, friends, and business associates. Some relied on me heavily as their therapist, others were less reliant. With two major exceptions, all the men relied on the group to serve as a home base, an ever-available safe haven to return to during times of stress and transformation.

Here are some of their stories.

GEORGE

It's a lot more fun to report successes. In many ways the work with George and his family was some of the most gratifying I've ever experienced. Through George's participation in the group, and through the subsequent sessions with just George and Sarah, both of them made remarkable progress in coping with some of the most vexing dilemmas confronted by contemporary couples.

Fairly early in one of the group sessions, George, who often was one of the more active participants, asked the group if he could talk about a recent conflict with Sarah. Up until that moment, that day's session had been freewheeling and unfocused. George had talked about the progress he and Sarah had made on a number of issues: her desire to take a promotion, the need for him to provide more child care, their conflicts over single versus dual checking accounts. They struggled to negotiate these issues, but a new issue had them baffled.

George: Sarah and I had a major blowout last week over a real trivial issue with our older daughter Kimberly. . . . I thought we were going to have World War III.

Gary: What happened?

George: Well, Kim was involved in her annual performance with the Cubbettes. . . .

Terry: What the hell are Cubbettes?

George: Oh, sorry. They're the girls' spirit squad for the boys' varsity teams. . . .

Terry: You mean those sweet little foxes with those dynamite body suits that. . . Oops, sorry man, no offense. As far as I'm concerned, that's fine entertainment.

That struck me as an interesting response by Terry. I made a note to return to the matter later.

George: See, that's part of the problem. Kim was chosen to do a solo number . . . quite an honor. . . . She was gonna do the big number from *Flashdance*. Have any of you guys seen the dance I'm talking about?

Chad: Are you kidding? Only about fifty or sixty times.

George: Then you know where I'm coming from. It's a pretty racy number, and I've gotta admit her costume's fairly tight and skimpy. That's actually what started the fight.

Gary: How's that?

George: Can't you guess? Sarah and the "little feminist," Stacy, my fourteen-year-old, went berserk when they saw the dress rehearsal. You gotta remember that Cubbettes have been a pretty touchy subject in our house anyways. Sarah hates the whole concept of young girls parading around in front of testosterone-crazed jocks.

Gary: By parading you mean dancing?

George: Yeah, they do dance numbers, but they also are a spirit squad. They make stuff for the ballplayers. . . . Kim and her mother have had some royal fiascoes about this. . . Sarah thinks it's demeaning to women. . . . Kim says her mother's being ridiculous just because she never did anything like that.

Gary: Where are you on this issue?

George: I'm in a tough spot. I understand Sarah's point, but I also think she's overreacting. Kim's had a pretty tough time the last few years. . . . She's always been borderline chubby. When she was twelve or thirteen she went through a real bad period where she was depressed all the time. She was real down on herself . . . hated her looks. . . . Funny thing, she's real bright and a great student and a talented musician; but she got into that "smart girls are nerds" thing for a while. . . . It was real hard for us. We even took her to a counselor.

Fred: What happened?

George: Here's where it gets interesting. Some of Kim's friends pressured her to go out for Cubbettes. As usual, she was convinced she wasn't good enough, but went out anyways. She made it— just barely, but she made it.

Fred: Good for her.

George: Yeah, well that turned things around for her. She really got into Cubbettes . . . took a lot of pride in being part of it . . . benefited greatly from the self-discipline, lost a bunch of weight, and really grew in self-confidence. Even Sarah admits that there's been a big difference in Kim.

Gary: So things had worked out well until this performance?

George: Not exactly. A lot better, but there still was tension. Stacy never let up . . . saw the whole thing as sexual exploitation. Sarah tolerated it, though she was real concerned about how it was affecting Kim.

Chad: I thought you said it was good for her?

George: Well it was, but Sarah said that Kim was getting obsessed with her appearance . . . you know, tons of makeup, always primping in front of mirrors, always dieting. Hell, she's thinner than all her friends now and she still thinks of herself as too fat.

Fred: Oh oh.

Gary: George, you know what I want to suggest here?

Terry and Chad: [*Chiming together*] Family meeting time.

George: [*Laughing*] Oh great, do we have to?

Gary: [*Smiling*] Your option.

George: Guess we need to.

Having pursued that far enough with George, I decided to get others involved in discussing the issue.

Gary: How about the rest of you guys? How do you line up on this issue?

Chad: That's the problem with this whole feminist thing. They're really trying to screw everything up. I guess they've got nothing better to do than protest everything.

Terry: Right, if a guy likes it, they're against it.

Paul: Hey, let's tell it like it is. They ain't gonna be happy until they've cut every man's balls off!

Fred: Oh God, don't let Paul get started again.

Gary: Seems like there's still strong feelings about not wanting to
lose a lot of traditional things.

The group laughed uproariously, making me realize what
I'd said.

Gary: No, that's not what I meant. Some traditional things should
be kept forever. But back to serious business for a minute. I'd
like to follow up on something Terry said.

Terry: What's that?

Gary: When you were talking about "young foxes" in leotards, you
apologized to George. What was that all about?

Terry: [*Looking surprised*] There you go, gettin' stupid again, Doc.
You don't call a guy's daughter a fox.

Gary: Why's that?

Terry: Shit, here we go again. Because a "fox" is *not* what you call a
guy's daughter. You don't dis somebody's family. What's wrong
with you, Doc?

Gary: Guess I'm really confused now. Isn't every "fox" some guy's
daughter? If calling her a fox is dissing her, are you saying it's
okay to do unless you know the father?

Fred: You guys got Doc going now. We're in for a ride now.

The rest of the session was spent exploring the strange contra-
diction in the male code about sexualizing and objectifying women.
The direct confrontation of the issue rattled and confused the
group members, making it possible for them to consider things in
a new light—the perspective of the objectified person (or objectified person's family member).

Later that month I met with George and Sarah.

Gary: Thanks for coming in again, Sarah.

Sarah: I'm happy to come. This whole therapy has been real helpful

to George and to both of us. I've got to confess that I had plenty
of misgivings about what good could come from a bunch of good
ol' boys sitting around together.

Gary: You weren't so sure about it?

Sarah: Not really. But it's gotten George thinking about things. He
used to just clam up. Now he comes home and actually starts
conversations himself. Amazing.

Gary: As you know from our phone conversation, George has been
working in the group on some issues about Kimberly.

George: Yeah, we've been talking about that little deal with Kim
and the Cubbettes.

Sarah: [*Making an unpleasant face*] George, I told you it's not a "little" deal with Kimberly, it's a "big" deal. It's about what our
daughters learn about the world. What could be any more
important than that?

George: OK, OK. It's a "big" deal. Why do you have to jump on
every word I use?

Sarah: It's not the words, George, it's the attitude—the lack of
importance that you attach to some issues.

George: Look, Sarah. Kim is doing better than she has in years. You
must admit that Cubbettes have been good for her.

Sarah: For heaven's sake, George. I didn't say that Kimberly wasn't
doing better. You're just trying to set this up as an argument you
can win.

George: That's a bunch of bull, Sarah!

The "discussion" seemed to be taking off from where we needed
to go right then, so I decided to refocus them.

Gary: Whoa, let's slow down for a minute. Let's take one issue at a
time. [*Sarah slid back in her chair looking somewhat relieved.*]
Sarah, you were starting to tell George about several issues that
were concerning you. Can you tell him what they are? George,
are you ready to hear what Sarah has to say?

Both gave nods of assent.

Sarah: The first big point is that this is not just about Kimberly and
Cubbettes. It's also about Stacy, and believe it or not, it's also
about Justin—you know, our sixteen-year-old "got-the-world-
by-the-tail, everything-is-cool" son.

George: Justin?

Sarah: Yes, Justin damn it. Mr. "No Sweat." But don't get me off
track. Stacy and Kimberly . . . don't you see that the issue isn't
some dumb dance group, but the whole thing about how these
girls think of themselves.

George: What's your point?

Sarah: The point is, can't you see what's happening to Kimberly?
Yes, she's better, she's not depressed all the time; but instead
she's gotten into a big beauty thing. She's always worried about
her looks. She's not studying. The other day she said she might
give up going to law school because it was too hard. She's talking about going to the Junior College where they have a better
social life and sports programs.

George: Don't we just want her to be happy?

Sarah: That's the point. Is happiness the ultimate objective? Look at
Justin: he's real happy; in fact he's so happy he's smug. He's playing football, got a sports car, and a string of one-night girlfriends.

George: Yeah, he's got a good life all right.

Sarah: Hello, George. Anybody home in there? You're totally
missing my point. He's living a totally selfish, narcissistic, self-
centered life. He uses people for what he wants, particularly
young girls. He's got three posters of half-naked women on his
walls, he gets girlie magazines, his favorite TV program is *Bay-
watch*. He's always making snide comments about bimbettes.

George: Oh, that.

Sarah: Yeah, oh that. I thought we'd gotten past that "boys will be
boys" stuff. I know that there's not much we can do now, but I

wish you wouldn't encourage him. At least make an effort to tell
him that you think there's more to life than pinups and recreational sex.

George became silent and thoughtful.

Gary: You seem pretty thoughtful, George. What are you thinking
    about?
George: Sarah's got a point. I've tried to say something, but I can't
    seem to pull it off. I'm not sure why.
Gary: Any ideas?
George: It's silly, but I'm probably afraid he'll think I'm some hope-
    less square. I guess I don't want him to lose respect for me.

We continued for a short time to explore how unrecognized
residuals of his masculine socialization had kept George from being
more active with his son. Later, we moved to the problems occurring between Justin and Stacy.

Sarah: Who can blame Stacy for jumping on Justin? He's impossible.
George: Now wait a minute, Sarah. Justin's not completely wrong
    here. Stacy has been on this "men are all pigs" kick since she
    got involved with that feminist action group at school . . . has
    that "all men are rapists" poster in her room . . . wears those
    weird boots and clothes. Every day she comes up with new out-
    rageous crap to get on Justin's case about. It gets a little old
    hearing that after a while.
Sarah: You've always been harder on Stacy.
George: [*Immediately, with considerable passion*] Goddamn it, Sarah,
    that's not true. I care very much about her. [*His voice quaked, his
    words became halting.*] I'm a member of that male species she's
    learning to hate. It kills me that she's pushing me away and
    won't give me a chance. [*He was overcome with tears and sobbing.*]

Visibly stunned by the pain she saw in George, Sarah reached over to grip his hand.

Sarah: I'm sorry, I didn't realize how much you were hurting. I've been afraid, too . . . afraid that my daughters would have to grow up with the same fears I had.

Having recognized each other's concerns, George and Sarah continued that day and for succeeding weeks to explore their hopes and fears for their children. Though their improved partnership was a little late in the parenting years, they nevertheless became much more united and supportive of each other. Over the next few months, follow-up sessions with the entire family further improved the family's commitment to working together in the struggle.

LUIS

For several months it had been touch and go with Luis. His work, always sporadic, had slowed dramatically. In fact, he was off work more days than he was on. Idleness had always taken a huge toll on Luis. The more he was at home, the more irritable he became. Tension had mounted between him and his stepchildren, and spilled over into heated conflicts with Mary. Finally, after a particularly stormy fight, he rushed out of the house and sought admission to the hospital, saying, "Nobody gives a damn about me. I sure as hell don't fit in around there. I'll just blow my fuckin' brains out!"

Although he was admitted to the hospital, he continued in the same group. In a session shortly after his admission, he spent lots of time voicing frustration about Mary's protective stance toward her children, and then again about his fears that Mary might become attracted to another man at her work site. His obsessive fears about losing Mary seemed to stand out—a logical area to explore further.

Gary: You know, Luis, it's pretty obvious that Mary is extremely important to you, so important that it's hard to stand the thought of others coming between you and her.

Luis: Of course, Mary is my life. Without her I wouldn't be here today.

Gary: How's that?

Luis: [*Looking at me puzzled*] Well, it's just the way it is. She's the only person that knows me, understands me. Hell, I don't trust any other motherfuckers out there. [*Looking around at the other guys in the group*] I don't mean you guys. You guys are different. It's just that it's a bad place out there.

Luis's relationship with Mary illustrated some of the more subtle aspects of the Centerfold Syndrome. Though not at all voyeuristic or objectifying of women's bodies, Luis had become deeply dependent upon Mary's emotional validation and physical comforting. He was utterly distrustful of men, seeing them all as potential adversaries for Mary's affections. So, one especially relevant group session for Luis began with group members exploring the role of fathers in their lives.

Gary: From what I'm hearing you guys say, there wasn't a lot of physical affection from your dads.

Paul: Not unless you count chokeholds and half-Nelsons.

Luis: Look, a father would have been nice, but don't get the wrong idea. I'm not saying I wanted to be babied. I never needed that hugging and holding crap.

Gary: So you never really cared about physical affection from your father?

Luis: [*With a distasteful facial expression*] No way!

Gary: [*Feigning surprise*] Really? Others? No physical affection from fathers, uncles, older men?

Several of them joined together in a chorus of boos and other sounds of disapproval. It seems that physical affection among men is a rather sensitive topic.

Terry: Shit, Doc. Would ya please get real! All we fuckin' need is a
bunch of guys going around hugging and holding each other like
a bunch of fuckin' fruits!

As is widely known, homophobia is ubiquitous among groups
of males. Tragically, many men are woefully intolerant of gay
lifestyles. Sadly, affection and tenderness among men is synony-
mous with sexuality.

I encouraged the group to continue talking about the aversive,
"unmanly" subject of the need for physical closeness. This touched
a nerve with Luis.

Luis: [*Clearing his throat repeatedly and clearly upset*] My mother was
the finest woman in the world—practically a saint. She nearly
worked herself to death trying to provide what she could for us
and keep the family together. She never asked for nothing for
herself and she always was there for me. One time our trailer
house was destroyed by a tornado and we lost the few things we
had. [*pausing to regain control of his tears*] Even lost my puppy
Blanco. Shit, I was just a kid . . . six or seven years old. I was
scared, upset. We had no place to go. [*He was crying.*]

Gary: Take your time, Luis.

Luis: It's just that I was really afraid and my mother knew exactly
how to make me feel safe. She could hold me, rock me, and sing
this little song. It made me know things would be okay.

The group was mesmerized by Luis's moving account of his
childhood trauma and by the dramatic contrast between that fearful child and the seemingly hardened adult they'd come to know.
George went over and gave Luis a few brief pats on the back.
Arthur offered a handkerchief. Luis suddenly became self-conscious
and returned to his more familiar self. He sat up, blew his nose into
his own handkerchief.

Luis: Hey, that was a long time ago. You get over that little kid crap.
You learn pretty fuckin' quick that you'd better grow up fast and

become a man. It's a damn hard world and there ain't no place for sissies.

The group went on to emphasize the need for men to prove their masculine toughness and deny their needs for intimacy and closeness. Men expect other men, whether allies or adversaries, to be ruggedly self-sufficient, emotionally and physically distant. Through sexuality, men allow women to get somewhat close, though not without experiencing considerable ambivalence. Behind their veneer of independence and self-sufficiency, many men like Luis become deeply reliant on the validation and physical comforting of a woman. Because men refuse to allow intimacy with other men, the dependence on women becomes even more pronounced.

At the close of the session, several members lingered for a few minutes. Fred, clearly moved by Luis's revelations seemed to want to say something. Instead, he put his hand on Luis's shoulder. Luis initially tensed up, but then relaxed some. Sensing acceptance of his overture, Fred gave Luis a tight and close embrace. The immediate reaction was amazing, as Fred's embrace generated a major tension release. Several group members laughed and enthusiastically hugged Luis, several hugged each other or patted each other on the back or shoulder. The dam of physical expression had been broken; the group had made a significant leap into tolerating intimacy. Luis commented upon it in the next session.

Luis: I need to say something about the last group. It was real hard for me to talk about those things. Everybody was real good to listen to me. It felt real good for people to accept me.

Gary: A good experience for you, Luis?

Luis: Yeah, it really is. See, over the past few years I ain't been trustin' nobody but Mary. I don't trust no guys. Mary's a good woman, but I can't rely on her all the time. It's real good to have some guys to talk to.

In his own way, Luis had identified one of the primary curative factors in a men's group and one of its principal roles in overcoming the Centerfold Syndrome. When men are able to be more intimate with one another, they can relate with women in a less intense and ambivalent fashion. Paradoxically, men can be less angry at women when they depend on them less.

ARTHUR

In many ways, Arthur was the most traditional man in the group. For that reason it was especially rewarding to see him grow beyond the narrow limitations of his sexual socialization. Socialized to objectify women's bodies, Arthur initially was emotionally paralyzed and totally unable to be of any help to a woman who had emotionally supported him for more than thirty years. Eventually, however, he was able to surmount his sexual conditioning and become a loving partner at a time when Faye needed him most.

Arthur's and Faye's crisis came to the forefront during an especially somber group session. Curious about the heavy atmosphere, I commented:

Gary: It seems kinda odd or weird in here today. Any ideas?
George: You could be right. Maybe we're just getting worn down by the constant struggles to figure things out.
Terry: Yeah. Too much analyzing is bad for your health.
Fred: Terry, you troublemaker, a little more introspection might save you some major headaches.

Fred paused and turned to Arthur, who had been sitting glumly, staring into space.

Fred: Actually, I've been somewhat concerned about you, Arthur. What's going on? You don't look so great.

Arthur didn't respond immediately, but eventually volunteered.

Arthur: Well, things have been pretty rough at my place lately. I'm
   not sure it's such a good idea to talk about it.
Fred: Come on, Arthur, you know damn well you need to talk when
   you're upset. Out with it.
Arthur: Well, I probably do need to get this off my chest. Ya see, last
   week Monique, my baby, jumped all over me.
Paul: Baby? You got a baby?
Arthur: No, Monique, my youngest—she's thirty-two now. I just call
   her baby cause she'll always be my baby girl. This was the first
   time she ever did me this way, so I know somethin' ain't right.
   You guys know that Faye's been sick, and we've been gettin' further and further apart lately.

Arthur's preoccupation with Faye's physical being had been so
pronounced that even several weeks after the surgery he was still
unable to acknowledge that Faye had had a breast removed.

Arthur: I'm spending more and more time outside the house at the
   club, and I ain't seen much of Faye or the girls. See, Monique
   caught me alone last week and started some stuff about me
   neglectin' her mother—even suggested I'd been spending too
   much with the sweet young things. She said that Mom has been
   hurtin' real bad and that I'd been letting her down. Well, that
   went all over me.

Arthur looked down at his feet and paused. The other members of the group waited expectantly as he moved his mouth without saying anything.

Gary: Go ahead, Arthur.
Arthur: Look, I love their mother. I would . . . [*He choked up before
   he could continue. After another pause to regain composure, he
   started again.*] I looked at Monique and tried to tell her, "Baby, I
   just don't know what to do. I'm real. . . ."

Arthur stopped again as his eyes filled with tears. The reality of Faye's mastectomy had hung over the group for several weeks. Partially because of their own discomfort with the issue and partially because of Arthur's reluctance to acknowledge it, group members left the topic alone, but they were able to rally to offer support.

Fred reached over to put his hand on Arthur's knee; Arthur smiled appreciatively. Chad and George had tears in their eyes. After a few minutes of painful silence, Arthur took several deep breaths, threw his head back to stare at the ceiling, and finally sat upright, half crying, half infuriated.

Arthur: Damn it all!

Luis: You gotta hang in there, man.

Terry: Don't you boys worry about the Ol' Lion. He'll be okay.

Arthur took out his handkerchief, wiped his eyes, and blew his nose.

Arthur: Thanks for the support. Hey, I *know* that Faye needs help, but it's very hard for me. How do I know what to do? I can hardly bear to think about what they did to her. I sure as hell can't talk about it or look at her. That's all she needs is me lookin' at her and getting sick. I mean, it just seems so weird or unnatural. I can't help but think of her like some sort of . . . of . . . [*He stopped himself.*]

Gary: It's okay, you can say it. Freak?

Arthur: [*Softly*] Yeah, it seems that way. I want to think about it different, but the idea keeps comin' to me. What in hell am I supposed to do?!

Fred: Arthur, take it easy. It's really natural to feel that way.

Arthur: Yeah, but that ain't all. Look, I'm a man with normal needs, so I ain't been so loyal lately. I can't resist the opportunities when they come, but I feel like a real low life when I mess around. [*He looked at the floor again.*] Monique and the girls have really lost respect for their ol' man.

Arthur's difficulty demonstrates an utterly sad and maddening outcome of the Centerfold Syndrome. He was unable to see his wife as a complete woman without her having both breasts.

Gary: Arthur, there are some things we can do about this.
Arthur: What's that?
Gary: Would you consider coming in with Faye to talk with me about this?

Arthur looked at me like I'd suggested he enter an Ironman Triathlon. He seemed to consider the matter before speaking.

Arthur: I'm not so sure about that one, Doc. It might be a bit too hard on Faye.
George: Hard on whom?
Fred: Arthur. You know you have to do that.
Luis and Chad: Gotta go for it, Arthur.

Arthur eventually agreed to the meeting. A time was set for the next week. As has often been the case, I had occasionally met Faye separately to keep her feeling involved with the treatment. My therapy plan often includes a mixture of group and family sessions.

In the first several minutes of our meeting, Arthur was nervous and talkative; Faye was reserved. After a period of reviewing the history of their relationship and complimenting them on their strengths, I nudged them toward their current crisis.

Gary: It sure sounds like you've had a marriage that's been pretty successful and has been able to weather its share of hard times.
Faye: [*Taking advantage of the opportunity*] We might as well tell him, Arthur; we haven't been much of a husband and wife lately.

Arthur shifted nervously, unaccustomed to talking openly about personal sexual matters.

Gary: Do you want to say more?

Faye: Yes, I really need to. Arthur, I know what's been going on. I hate it! I can't take it any more!

A look of horror came over Arthur's face, but before he could say anything, Faye continued with a low and quivering voice.

Faye: I know how bad I've been. I've been a terrible wife. I've prayed for strength, but I haven't been heard. God has punished me. I've been a miserable, carping, unhappy shrew. I've let you down, Arthur, and I feel horrible. I'm a very bad person who is a disgrace to her family.

Though she seemed to want to blurt out more vicious self-criticism, Faye, overcome with pain, moaned and buried her head in her hands, crying inconsolably.

Arthur was dumbstruck by Faye's outburst. He moved quickly to her and held her for several minutes as she sobbed. As he rocked her he kept repeating, "It's not you, baby, it's not you, baby." Arthur tried to find a way to tell Faye of his own anguish, of his failure to be of help. But Faye continued.

Faye: I know I'm not a woman anymore. I know how repulsive I am. I know you have needs that I haven't met. All men want to be with "complete" women.

Although I knew of the phenomenon in which a victim blames herself for her suffering, it was nevertheless horrifying to actually witness how Faye, already scarred, castigated herself for the disintegration of the marriage. Arthur was deeply pained by Faye's distress, but taken aback by her self-blame, and unsure about how to help her.

Gary: It seems pretty clear how deeply fearful you've both been for Faye's safety. But now that she's more secure, you're both trying to deal with something much more complex—ideas about who Faye is, who she's been, what she needs to be, and what she can still be. I wonder if it might be useful for us to spend some time talking about your loss, as well as what you've both believed sexuality is all about.

Over the next several weeks, Arthur and Faye worked together, and separately, to examine the role of sexuality in their lives. Faye acknowledged her long-standing concern that she would be able to continue to be attractive to Arthur as she aged. Arthur confessed that he had had great difficulty managing his physical responses to attractive women, especially to large-breasted women. Both tried to face their grief—Faye over the loss of a sense of completeness, Arthur over his loss of a sexual stimulus. Gradually, Faye began to discover a reservoir of resentment about the way Arthur related with her sexually, about how his objectification of her body had set the stage for problems and about how his fascination with her breasts made it difficult for him to know *her*. Arthur was surprised to realize the pain he had caused, but once again he was unsure about what to do.

Gary: Arthur, you've been taken in by a society that teaches men to get hung up on women's physical characteristics, to objectify them. Both Faye and you have been badly burned by this. Let's see what we can do to get past it.

Space doesn't permit my providing extensive details about all that's involved in trying to deal with the losses of mastectomy. Together, and with the help of support groups, Faye and Arthur worked through the difficult stages of adjustment—visual confrontation, desensitization, and accommodation—talking about the interaction between visual and sensual aspects of sexuality. To a large extent, Arthur worked to develop new habits of perception—literally to *look at Faye in a totally new way*. He tried to see Faye as a caring, loving, and sensual person, instead of as a pair of breasts with a person attached. As they made progress in this endeavor, Faye and Arthur became more able to substitute an intimate sexuality for an objectified visual one.

There were interesting repercussions from Arthur's efforts to overcome the Centerfold Syndrome. In his family, he became more compassionate with his daughters, more understanding of their efforts to juggle the cultural pressures on women. For a brief time he became locked in conflict with his only son, Arthur, Jr. Although I didn't witness the actual encounter, I later learned about an interesting interaction between father and son. Arthur had become increasingly uneasy with his son's womanizing and his constant playing of heavily sexual rap videos. Tension mounted as Arthur rode Junior, about the videos and about his disrespect for women. Tiring of his father's nagging, Junior finally responded.

Junior: What the "F" has gotten into you anyways? You used to be pretty smooth, but you've gotten so old and uptight lately.

Enraged by his son's outburst, Arthur grabbed him by the shoulders and shook him, nearly losing his temper. Before that happened, he calmed himself, took his hands off his son and started walking around the room.

Arthur: Son, I guess I need to remember that you ain't got any idea what's been goin' on with me and your mother. I need to tell you about some things that I've been thinking about lately.
Junior: Oh God. Get me outta here.
Arthur: No, it's gonna be all right. We can talk this out.

In a single, simple interaction, I saw cause for hope. If fathers could teach their sons, maybe there could eventually be a generation of men free of the Centerfold Syndrome.

FRED

It's hard to categorize Fred's experience. In some notable ways he realized the need to change problematic patterns and initiate some important changes. Before long, however, he was victimized by the widespread barrier to intimacy among men.

For the first time Fred missed a group session without giving any clear indication why. Since he hadn't missed very often, there was considerable curiosity regarding his whereabouts.

Gary: Anybody got an idea what happened to Fred?

George: Got me. Thought he was gonna be here this week. Come to think of it though, he was fairly upset at the end of the group last week.

Chad: Yeah, I noticed that, too. He took off like a bat outta hell . . . weird for him. Usually he hangs around for a while . . . you know, visits and stuff.

Mike: I hope he's okay. He's been pretty cool. I like having him here.

Gary: I appreciate your saying that, Mike. It hasn't always been easy for you to relate to people. You and Fred seemed to get along well.

Mike: [*After pausing for a moment, seeming somewhat emotional*] That's really true. I guess in some ways he's seemed like kind of an uncle for me. Sorta reminds me of my Uncle Lou.

Gary: Uncle Lou?

Mike: You guys remember him, don't you? My father's brother. He's the one that kinda did stuff with me as a kid when my dad had no use for me.

George: I remember you talking about him. He was real important to you . . . [*noticing that Mike has gotten noticeably upset*] but anyway, that was another time. You haven't heard at all from Fred have you?

Mike: No, I haven't. That's a little creepy, since he sometimes calls me to do stuff.

At that point I couldn't help but notice as Terry looked at Luis and made a strange face. Not sure what that was about, I let it slide for the moment.

Arthur: Guess when you get old like us you never know. Say, Mike, whadda you and Fred do anyhow?

Mike: Hey, nothin' special. Sometimes we listen to music, sometimes we go out for coffee—whatever.

At this point Luis and Terry started getting restless again. Luis seemed to signal something to Terry, but Terry shook his head negatively, pointing at Luis. This seemed to be getting fairly distracting, so I looked to Luis expectantly.

Luis: It looks like nobody ain't gonna say nuthin', so I'll just go ahead. See, me and Terry and Arthur were talking after the last group and . . . well, I ain't too sure how to say this. . . . See, we don't want to hurt anybody, but it wouldn't be right for anybody to get hurt either. We been thinking about Mike and wantin' to be sure everything is okay.

Mike: [*Surprised and somewhat upset*] What do you mean? What's the problem?

Luis: It's no problem with you, Mike. We just don't want to see anything bad happen.

Mike: I'm really confused here. What do you mean?

Terry: Let me go ahead and say it. We just don't want to see Fred put no moves on you.

Mike: [*Stunned and upset*] Moves? What are you guys talking about?

Terry: Well, it's like this. I know it ain't right to talk about a guy when he ain't here, but we gotta talk about this. Some of us have begun to wonder a little bit about Fred . . . you know, he ain't married or nuthin' . . . no girlfriends . . . plus he kinda gives you the idea that maybe he ain't exactly like the rest of us . . . you know what I mean?

George: Terry, are you saying that you think Fred is gay?

Terry: I don't know . . . just wonderin'.

George: [*Raising his voice*] Hell, who knows. Frankly, I'm not sure what difference that makes.

Terry: Hey, relax. We just don't wanna see anybody get hurt. You know Mike ain't exactly the most experienced guy in the world.

Mike: You guys are really wrong about Fred. He's a great guy. I told you he's kinder to me than anybody ever has been. Why are you saying those things?

The remainder of the group time was spent in heated disagreement about how to handle this divisive issue. Mike was angry and hurt. George and Chad were defensive of Fred, feeling that he'd been badly mistreated. Arthur, Luis, and Terry became angry that others didn't appreciate their efforts to "protect" Mike. The personal feelings were intense. We were suddenly confronting one of men's most difficult issues—homophobia.

Fred came to the next group meeting. The tension in the room was extreme. After a few moments of silence, Fred began.

Fred: I felt that it was important that I come back this week, partially for Mike's sake, but for myself also. The past few weeks have been a real nightmare for me.

Though his voice was calm, it was clear that Fred was struggling to maintain his composure.

Fred: This year has been real hard. Several things have piled up . . . been increasingly estranged from my kids. My sixtieth birthday is on the horizon. The teaching has been mundane . . . but mostly I think it's been the loneliness that's been wearing me down.

He paused for a few minutes. The room was totally silent. George, Chad, and Mike watched Fred intently. Luis and Arthur studied the floor. Terry stared off into space.

Fred: It's been hard, but I've felt like I needed to keep trying to fight off the depression I sometimes slip into. Frankly, this group has been a big source of support for me. The people in here have been my social network lately. This is in spite of the fact that I've never felt completely safe or accepted here. People know too little about me, and I guess I've been too cowardly to open up about it.

He looked directly at Terry, who gave him a quick glance before looking away.

Fred: [*Sighing deeply*] I've been living a more openly gay life style now for several years. You never know exactly where you can be open and where you have to stay closeted. I'd dearly hoped that I could be open and honest in here. Sure, I've been aware of the homophobia. I can't ignore the "fag" and "queer" references, but I'd hoped that we might somehow get past that. I missed the group a week ago because the gay bashing the previous week was pretty intense and I wasn't up to it again last week.

George: So that's why you didn't come.

Fred: [*Smiling weakly*] Yes, childish I guess. I figured a week off might help me figure out what to do about the issue. Well, ironically it actually did.

Gary: How's that?

Fred: I guess I should be grateful to Terry and Luis for being honest enough to bring the issue up . . . but I must tell you . . . I've never been more disappointed and frustrated. [*His voice trembled.*] Mike has been like a little brother, maybe in some ways like a son to me. It was deeply hurtful to me that people would construe my affection for that young man as a cheap sexual overture, an attempt to seduce him. That really is more than I can stand. I'm afraid that I cannot ever feel comfortable in here again.

There were several minutes of silence. George and Chad seemed to be struggling to find the right thing to say. The silence of Luis, Arthur, and Terry was oppressive.

Fred: [*Calmly again*] Before I go, I need to say a few more things. I've gained a lot from being in this group. One ironic thing . . . once upon a time I might have tried to seduce someone like Mike. We've talked a lot in here about lust and women's bodies. Well, I know about lust, although for me, it's not *women's* bodies. For several years I was one of the biggest chasers of attractive bodies you'll ever see. Just like a lot of others, it was a big challenge to me to try to score, and be seen with, the most gorgeous hunk you could. . . . Chad and Terry, in many ways we've had a lot in common.

Chad: That's amazing. I've never thought about it that way.

Terry didn't respond, but fidgeted, started tapping his foot.

Fred: Yes, it can be the same, gay or straight. Objectifying a person has the same cost—alienation and spiritual numbing—but I'm making progress with that now. No more relationships with people I don't know or care about . . . no more trying to show off at a gay bar with your latest score. In fact, sex doesn't seem that critical to me anymore. Forced to choose between sex without intimacy or intimacy without sex, it's not even close . . . I'll take the intimacy.

Gary: So closeness and friendship have become more important to you.

Fred: Yes, that's the bitter irony. My relationship with Mike had no sexual overtones whatever. Mike needed a friend; so did I.

Mike: We can still be friends, can't we?

Fred: I don't know why not.

Gary: Would you consider coming back sometime in the future?

Fred: We'll have to wait and see.

As Fred rose to leave, George, Mike, Chad, and I also rose to embrace him.

Over the next few weeks the group struggled to process the myriad of feelings stirred up by Fred's departure. George and Chad initially blamed Terry and Luis, but ultimately came to recognize how they too had allowed homophobia to affect their interactions with Fred and others. Fred's comments about the need for intimacy sparked considerable discussion. Terry held firm to his conviction that he'd rather die than give up sex, but Chad and George became even more convinced that they had more intimacy needs than they had realized. I encouraged the group members to talk about how comfortable they could be getting close to each other, how much intimacy was possible between men. With the exception of Terry, who remained adamant that men shouldn't get emotionally or physically close, all agreed that emotional closeness, and even some physical closeness, was possible and useful for men. The group continued to talk about trying to persuade Fred to come back to the group.

CHAD

When he entered the group, Chad believed that he loved women. He came to realize, however, that what he loved was an artificial and hollow image of women. Over several months he came to confront that reality, ultimately replacing superficial with substantive, visual with intimate, illusory with genuine.

Having been out of town for three days, I didn't check my office answering machine until late one Sunday evening. I was startled to hear a message from Chad saying he was in the locked psychiatric unit. I was to learn later that he had taken an overdose of antidepressant medications after a binge of alcohol and cocaine. When I visited him at the hospital, I found him to be worn and pale, but in better spirits than I had expected. After several minutes of small talk, we got down to business.

Gary: So, what's this all about, Chad?

Chad: Good question. I've certainly had plenty of time over the last few days to consider that issue myself.

Gary: Come up with anything?

Chad: Actually, I think I've gotten several ideas. There have been a number of things that have been eating at me. You may remember that I said a long time ago that the band routine was getting to me . . . different gigs, different babes, constant change. Weird thing about it was that, though I was living my dream, being with the most fantastic looking women I'd ever imagined—you name it: tall ones, short ones, big breasts, long legs—all real horny and hot-to-trot. Millions of guys would kill to get the broads I was getting.

Gary: I remember you talking about that.

Chad: Yeah, well the pattern continued. Funny thing was that though the bodies were different, the routine was the same. They'd come on to me. We'd get together and start getting it on. I'd tell her how great her body looked, how sexy she was. She'd do these wild sexual antics, you know, screaming, writhing, moaning, that type of stuff. When we got worn out, she'd tell me I was the greatest she ever had. Doc, does it make sense to you that I'd *always* be the best they'd had?

Gary: Seems to be a stretch of the imagination.

Chad: Well, it is, but I guess I tried to make the stretch cause I sorta bought it for a while. Actually considered myself the world's most talented lover. But anyways, that was bugging me, but it wasn't what set off this episode.

Gary: What was that?

Chad: It was a tiny thing really. Remember when George was talking about his daughter?

Gary: Kimberly?

Chad: Yeah. He was saying that he and Sarah had talked about their fears that she would end up attracting some "low life" that was primarily interested in her as a sex object. Well, I may have imagined this, but I could swear that George glanced at me when he talked about this low-life scumbag. Did you see that?

Gary: Not sure. What did you make of this?

Chad: This bothered me then, but really started to get all over me during the next week. Hell, I admire George. I look up to him. He's got his stuff together: good career, married to a great lady. She don't take no shit, but that's okay, too. In a way, that's pretty great.

Gary: What do you mean?

Chad: She's got a mind and a personality . . . like she's a real person . . . not playing games.

Gary: That appeals to you?

Chad: Sure as hell does . . . more and more. Seems like she really cares about their relationship. It ain't just an act. Plus, he's got a neat family. I had sorta hoped that I might get that stuff some-day myself.

Gary: You're not sure now?

Chad: That's what scared the hell outta me. I mean, I think people associate me with Terry. I mean, that guy needs help. He's got no respect for women. I always saw myself as different. I always thought I treated women with respect; but now I wonder.

Gary: So that was bugging you?

Chad: Not only that though. The deal with Fred really put the cap-per on it for me. Look, I can see that Fred is different in that he's gay and all that, but he was right. He and I are very much alike in terms of relationships . . . always chasing the newest piece of ass, trying to feel good by being seen with some gor-geous babe, didn't really know anybody real close . . . that whole thing bummed me out. I started seeing myself as an old man with nobody in my life.

Gary: That got to you?

Chad: Yeah, seemed like the bottom just dropped out for me. I don't drink and do drugs, but I just felt this urge to get totally fucked

up—went on a tear and ended up here. You don't suppose this
was one of those "cry for help" deals, do you?

Gary: You tell me.

Even though he'd had a rough few weeks, Chad was now feeling much better. He'd recognized some self-destructive patterns,
and although he hadn't yet corrected them, he seemed to have a
better perspective on relationships.

A few months later, he had an interesting story to tell.

Chad: I've got some things I want to tell the group about—that
okay?

Terry: Go for it.

Chad: There's this kinda strange thing happening right now that I
want to get people's ideas about. About two months ago I
started spending more time with my sister Debra. She's two
years older than me, but we used to have a great relationship,
till I got so into babes and music.

Terry: Right, Mr. Sex, Drugs, and Rock and Roll.

Chad: Except hold the drugs. Well, that time in the psych unit got
me really thinking about my way of being with women. I figured
that since I wanted to try something new, I'd get in touch with
my sister again. You know, a relationship where you don't have
to think about getting laid.

Terry: I may never understand you, man.

Chad: You might if you listen to what I'm saying. Well, I started
having this great time with Debra. It was really fun—sharing
our ideas and thoughts, going places, doing things. I never really
missed the sex that much.

Terry: I'm listenin', but I sure ain't hearin' it yet.

Chad: Now it gets even more unusual. Debra has this friend Phyllis.
I've sorta known about her for a while, but never paid much
attention to her. She's chubby, plain, not much to look at.

George: No wonder you didn't notice her—certainly not *your* type.

Chad: That's what I figured . . . but life has really taken a strange
turn. Phyllis went along with us on some of our outings. Well,
the chemistry was fantastic. She's got a great sense of humor,
she's unbelievably sharp, practically knows what I'm thinking,
has incredible opinions about things. We'd talk about stuff for
hours.

Terry: Don't tell me this. I can't stand it.

George: Shut up, Terry.

Chad: Debra started seeing her boyfriend again, but Phyllis and
I kept seeing each other. It was amazing how much we
enjoyed doing stuff together. Well, about two weeks into
this I noticed that I was getting really turned on, wanted
to have sex with her. I asked her and she was pretty interested, too.

George: And?

Chad: It was really nice—a really different kind of experience. We
talked, joked, and laughed *even during sex.* That was strange for
me. After I came we talked and cuddled for a couple of hours.
That was really different, too—real nice.

Gary: Pretty different from usual for you?

Chad: *Real* different. I mean, we actually look into each other's eyes
when we make love. It feels real close and tender—makes me
feel a lot different afterwards.

Gary: Different?

Chad: Yeah, close and sorta *with* her, not somewhere else—at least,
most of the time.

Chad had make a significant breakthrough in discovering sexuality springing from intimacy rather than from conditioned sexual responses to anonymous women. But was he "home free?"
Would old habits and socialization pressures disappear that easily
and automatically?

Gary: Say more.

Chad: Sometimes I find myself feeling a little scared, putting up walls. But she notices that . . . mentions it, and we talk about it, usually get it worked out.

George: What do you mean *usually?*

Chad: There's one issue that's been bugging me. George, maybe you could give me some ideas how to handle it.

George: Glad to try.

Chad: You guys remember I said that Phyllis is chubby? She is, heavy, not very big breasts, and her bottom is sorta flabby. I hate talking about this, but I can't help but notice. Once I noticed feeling a tiny bit self-conscious being seen with her around the guys. George, I don't know Sarah, but you've said that she isn't physically perfect. How do you deal with that? Anybody got any ideas?

Terry: You don't wanna hear my thoughts.

George: It's not easy, Chad. Seems to me that there's a big deal made of what attractive is supposed to be. Sarah and I have talked about it a lot . . . especially after the time I made the joke about my "lucky" friend whose wife got breast implants for his birthday. I haven't solved it, but we've made progress.

Chad: How?

George: For one thing, it seems to be partly a matter of learning to look at Sarah differently, sorta not looking at the little physical details, but seeing the entire person. It's hard to explain.

It *is* hard to explain, but George did a good job of putting his finger on the issues. The group spent considerable time over the next few weeks talking about how sex and beauty affected their relationships with women. Some of them talked frankly about the need to get past their hangups with centerfold women, others thought the entire discussion was absurd. Chad, to his credit, continued to wrestle successfully with his sexual conditioning. He ultimately achieved a deeply rewarding relationship with a woman who was not his physical "dream woman," but was a woman who could make his days and nights stimulating and meaningful.

●   ●   ●   ●

Each man had his own issues and each made his own changes. Overall, Fred, George, Chad, Arthur, and Luis made considerable progress in overcoming differing aspects of the Centerfold Syndrome. Unfortunately, not all the men did as well. Their stories are next.

6

MEN WHO'VE MADE LITTLE PROGRESS

For some men, the Centerfold Syndrome maintains a powerful hold. Many of them recognize their troubles, but find change very difficult to accomplish. Others never see the problems.

MIKE

Unlike some men, who displace their pain onto others, Mike bore the full brunt of his sexual distress. The group helped him uncover his symptoms and encouraged him to change. Unfortunately, change did not come easily for Mike.

Even though he always attended the sessions, Mike remained more or less on the fringes of the group. Sometimes I thought he was beginning to assimilate, but other times I was convinced that he was completely out of touch. However, just when I would be ready to give up hope that he'd gain anything, he'd come up with some indication that he was tuned in and getting a great deal from the chance to meet with the others. Unfortunately, his extreme social anxiety seemed to make it hard for him to share much personal information. His private life, especially his sexuality, remained a relative mystery until one week, when I received a call from Fred, who had been outside of the group for a few months.

Fred reported that he had been doing fairly well himself, and that he had actually considered giving the group another shot. His reason for calling, however, was Mike. Apparently Fred had continued to see Mike somewhat regularly, sort of mentoring him about the ways of the world. As their friendship grew and Mike became more comfortable with Fred and less guarded about his private life, Fred visited him at his apartment. While there, Fred discovered Mike's secret "hobby" of collecting pornographic magazines and videos. Though Fred only saw a small portion of the collection, he was concerned enough to ask Mike to talk with me about it. When I talked to Mike, he became very upset and began crying. He said he was really scared, but would talk about the problem in an individual session. We scheduled such a meeting during the next week.

It took considerable time to get Mike comfortable enough to talk about his pornography habit, but eventually he was able to break the ice.

Mike: I guess I ought to get around to talking about the dirty
   books, huh?

Gary: If you feel ready to do that. Is this something that upsets you?

Mike: Not always. Sometimes I don't think about it, but sometimes I
   feel real guilty, kinda disgusted with myself, real dirty.

Gary: Tell me a little bit about it, Mike. What's this all about?

Mike: I guess I'm not too sure myself. Fred thought this was kind of a
   problem. I guess I agreed with him. See, I sorta have this collection of magazines and videos . . . been getting them for a few
   years.

Gary: You mean a lot of them?

Mike: [*Looking ashamed*] Yeah, several hundred I guess. They stack
   up and I really can't let go of them.

Gary: That's a lot of money, I'd guess.

Mike: Yeah, I probably spend most of my check on stuff. I've got
   subscriptions to *Playboy* and *Penthouse* and a couple others. Plus
   the Playboy video club. It's a lot of cash, I guess.

Gary: Is it the money that's been bothering you the most?

Mike: Well, it used to be, but lately, since I've been in the group, I've been thinking that it's kinda weird. I think about stopping, but I can't seem to . . . you know what I mean?

Gary: I'm not sure, Mike. What is it you want to stop?

Mike: Well, spending all that money . . . [*He paused.*] Plus, I guess the other stuff, too.

Gary: Other stuff?

Mike paused for several minutes, trying to decide how to continue.

Mike: I guess you could say I spend a lot of time, ah . . . Guess you could say . . . sorta playin' with myself . . . you know . . . jerkin' off.

Gary: A lot?

Mike: Yeah, gets to be a bunch . . .

Gary: A bunch?

Mike: Yeah. Sometimes three or four times a day. Sometimes just once . . . depends on the circumstances.

Mike went on to describe a pattern of compulsive masturbation that had been going on for several years. He eventually admitted that he'd masturbate two or three times with the arrival of each new magazine or video. As the habit became more pervasive, he found himself doing little else. Though he'd had social opportunities, he generally passed them up, preferring to stay at home with his magazines and videos.

Gary: So you got pretty isolated because of your porno habit?

Mike: Guess so. It just seemed easier . . . except I felt kinda . . . I don't know . . . I guess kinda perverted.

Gary: Tell me what you mean, Mike.

Mike: Well, it was sorta strange. During the day I'd be thinking about getting home and getting alone. I'd get pretty excited thinking about it. . . . There were these two girls that worked at the bank that really got me going. One of them looked just like one of last year's Playmates of the Year . . . same color hair, same shape legs. I couldn't tell for sure, but her breasts seemed to be about the same. Guess I spent a lot of time picturing her without clothes . . . couldn't stop looking at her.

Gary: Did you know her?

Mike: Oh God, no. I'd get real panicky being near her. Besides, she kinda wasn't too fond of me.

Gary: Oh?

Mike: Yeah, she went to my boss complaining that I was staring at her. . . . You know, watching her all the time.

Gary: So this has created job problems for you?

Mike: I guess it has. But that's not what's really getting to me. It seems that the whole thing is becoming, ah . . . I guess it's depressing. I feel that it's not as much excitement. . . . I really feel down afterwards now. I'm not sure I want to feel this way anymore.

I saw Mike several times individually, to supplement his group experiences. We explored the origins of his insecurities and sexual attitudes. He talked about his highly religious parents, who thought of Mike as very disappointing to them. Their sexual attitudes were extremely conservative. Once, when discovering one of Mike's magazines, they threatened to throw him out of the house unless he could improve his morals.

As he discussed the issues, Mike came to recognize that his pornography habits were seriously interfering with his life. Committed to change, he disposed of all his magazines and videos and pledged to work on developing a healthier relationship with women. Unfortunately, he underestimated the power of his habit. Within three months he admitted to the group that he had begun buying "just one or two" magazines.

Gary: Mike, you said coming in that you had something to talk to the group about.

Mike: I guess I do . . . but it's not real easy.

Gary: Take your time.

Mike: See, it's about the porno stuff. You guys know . . . my porno habits?

Terry: You know, I never really understood what's the big friggin' deal. Who's getting all bent out of shape about a few fuck books? Hell, nobody ever got hurt by those things.

Mike looked at Terry, trying to respond, but wasn't sure how to proceed.

Mike: [*In a low voice*] I'm not so sure of that.

Terry: What are you driving at, man?

Gary: Mike, why don't you try to tell the group more about what you've been trying to deal with. Terry, give Mike a chance to explain something that's been causing him a lot of pain. Try to keep an open mind about this.

Terry: OK, OK . . . take it easy, will ya?

After several minutes of fumbling for the right words, Mike was able to tell the group about his compulsive use of pornography and his compulsive masturbation. Gradually, Terry and other skeptics began to get the picture.

Terry: OK, so you got a little carried away with it. So just quit; stop buying the shit and be done with it.

Mike: [*Visibly distressed*] But that's just it . . . I can't stop it!

Mike paused for several minutes before continuing in a low, flat voice.

Mike: I did all right for a while, but it didn't last. I started to go by the stores . . . started to fantasize about what was in the magazines . . . kept getting all worked up . . . couldn't keep my reactions under control. I finally broke down and bought some.

The group members were stunned to realize how powerfully Mike had been taken over by his pornography habits. They tried to offer support.

Chad: Maybe you're overreacting, Mike. Maybe a couple won't hurt anything.
Mike: But that's the problem. I can't seem to get enough of them. And the worst part is how I feel after I use them.
George: How's that, Mike?
Mike: It's hard to say . . . real dirty . . . real sick. I hate feeling like a sex pervert all the time.

The group continued to offer moral support to Mike and to encourage him to fight to overcome his pornography habits. He's continuing the struggle.

PAUL

Throughout the history of the group, Paul had been one of the more angry members. In many ways, it seems he primarily used the group as an outlet for his rage against women. This emotional ventilation can be helpful in itself, but it leads to even greater progress when a man can see his own role in the creation of problems. Anger at women, though very common in men, cannot be an end point. It needs to be replaced with a more complex understanding of the situational stresses confronted by men *and* women.

Groups are particularly helpful when they help a man uncover the myriad of painful emotions that often lies beneath his anger. Improved emotional insight helps men recognize self-defeating patterns and change them into behaviors more likely to provide satisfying relationships. Unfortunately, the process of self-examination is an arduous one, and many men revert to old habits to relieve their discomfort. Paul was one of those men.

Paul started missing sessions, an unusual pattern for him. More puzzling was his changed demeanor when he did come to the group. Several members noticed the change and were curious.

Chad: Paul, you sure seem to be in better spirits. What's the deal?
Paul: Beats me. Must be the new job I just got. A few bucks improves my outlook on life . . . besides, it keeps Elaine from bugging me about child support.
Terry: Elaine? So that's her name. I always thought her name was "that fucking bitch."

The group laughed. Terry and others pressed, but Paul was resolute about there being no change in his life. It didn't compute. Paul was markedly different, but he couldn't identify anything to account for his new attitude. Late in the session, however, we learned a lot more about the factors underlying his improved mood and outlook, when he made a casual reference to "Kristi."

Paul: That's true. Kristi's son Josh is a lot like that.

Several group members turned to look at Paul quizzically.

Terry: Who the hell is Kristi?
Paul: [*Somewhat taken aback*] Kristi? Oh, she's this girl that works at the shop where I just started.
Terry: Yeah?
Paul: Yeah what?
George: Well, who is she? Give a few precious details here.
Paul: It's no big thing. She's a young parts clerk that I been talking to a little bit lately.
Terry: Just talkin', huh? You sure you ain't holdin' out a touch here?
Paul: No, she's a pretty decent young lady. Been through hell though . . . 'bout seven months ago she divorced the "no-good low life" she was married to. The prick treated her pretty bad.

Left her with the three-year-old, never paid her nuthin'. He better not let me run into him.

Terry: Well, what about the other pertinent facts? She a fox? How
old? You know what I mean.

Paul: She's young . . . about eighteen, but pretty mature. She's a
pretty little thing [*holding his hand five feet or less off the floor*].

Chad: Hey, good deal.

Gary: Paul, I'm a bit confused. Is this a relationship or just talking,
or what?

Paul: Both, I guess.

As has often been the case, I was surprised at how little insight
many men have about the role of relationships in their well-being.
It seems that as a way of defending against emotional involvement
and fears of losing control, some men deny the importance of their
relationships, both to others and to themselves.

Gary: Well, when were you going to get around to telling us about
her?

Paul: Oh, I don't know. I'm not sure it's that big a deal . . . didn't
wanna take up group time with it.

Gary: Come on, Paul. Are you serious? Do you really see this as a
small thing? Are you seeing much of her?

Paul: Well, I stay at her place every so often. I went to the park with
her and her kid the last few Sundays.

Terry: You're gettin' in plenty deep on that one, man.

The session ended before we were able to pursue the subject
much further. We agreed to talk about it more in the following session, but Paul didn't come. No one had heard from him for several
weeks when I got a call from a nervous-sounding young person with
a meek voice.

Kristi: This is Kristi. I need to talk with you about Paul. I know that
he goes to your group.

She apparently didn't know that he hadn't been attending lately.

Gary: Nice to talk with you. What's going on?
Kristi: I've been wanting to call you for a long time. I wasn't sure it would be all right. I've been worried about Paul. Things haven't been going so great for a while. He's starting to get touchier and touchier about silly stuff . . . about who I talk to and stuff like that. I need you to tell me if I'm doing something wrong? Why does Paul get so angry and so possessive? He goes crazy when I mention somebody I used to date or somebody who talks to me. How should I deal with this?

I tried to get Paul and Kristi to come into the office to talk about their relationship. Kristi was eager, but Paul resisted. It became clear that Paul, with very little insight, had chosen to repeat a destructive relationship pattern rather than make substantive changes in his way of relating with women. By choosing a younger, physically small, and psychologically immature partner, he was able to temporarily restore his lost sense of control. This was a very risky choice, as Kristi's most innocent efforts to relate with others were enough to alarm Paul. Trouble loomed for the relationship, but I could not do much except encourage her to call if she ever wanted help for herself. Perhaps if she did call, the suffering of her previous relationship could be averted.

A few weeks later I got the phone call I had feared. Kristi's father was calling to tell me that she was at her parents' home after a major fight with Paul. Apparently Paul had become incensed about Kristi's secretiveness, had searched her purse, and had found the phone number of a person named Chris. Despite Kristi's pleas that Chris was a girlfriend, Paul started screaming, broke a lamp, and eventually grabbed Kristi by the throat and threatened to kill her if he ever found another phone number in her purse.

I spent considerable time helping Kristi and her parents develop an appreciation of the seriousness of Paul's violence potential, and helping them develop an appropriate strategy for dealing with that violence and ensuring Kristi's safety.

Once I was comfortable that Kristi and her parents were on the right track, I made efforts to contact Paul. After several days, I finally reached him.

Gary: Paul, the group and I have been real concerned about you.
    How about coming in to talk?
Paul: I'm fine. What's the big deal?
Gary: Paul, I'm concerned about your relationship with Kristi and
    I'm not sure you're handling things real well right now. How
    about we get together?
Paul: Look, Doc. I appreciate you calling, but I got everything under
    control. Sure, Kristi's playin' the same games as Elaine, but I can
    handle it.

Paul continued to stonewall and deny the need for help. I pleaded with him to try to see the repeating patterns and consider returning to treatment, but he continued to resist.

TERRY

We simply never got very far with Terry. At times he was willing to drop his guard and tell us a little about his past.

Terry: My old man was like lots of others—never around. He
    worked for the railroad. What I saw of him didn't amount to
    much. He did do some shit with my older brothers, but he never
    paid much attention to me. Hell, nobody was ever really sober
    around there. When the ol' man got drunk, which was all the
    fuckin' time, he'd said I wasn't really his kid anyways.
Paul: Well, fuck him!
Terry: No shit.

Gary: Sounds pretty rough.

Terry: Actually, it wasn't all bad. The ol' man was always bringin' his girlfriends around. He made it clear that he'd slice up any-body who touched his current woman, but shit, how would he know? There was plenty of pussy available all the time. I was one giant step ahead of all the other dudes. Shit, by the time I was eleven, I'd seen every skin flick there was. I knew hundreds of ways to get laid, and even invented a few myself. Everybody around knew I was the number one stud in the neighborhood.

Terry described a fairly traumatic childhood environment that, tragically, isn't totally alien to many young men. For him, women became tools and sex became a form of revenge. Sexual conquests were a badge of manhood.

We pressed Terry about times he may have experienced inti-macy or emotional compassion.

George: Terry, didn't I get the idea once that you were pretty tight with that one chick . . . what was her name? Cassandra?

Terry: [*Suddenly emotional*] Yeah, that fucked-up bitch. Had my kid . . . tried to fuck me over . . . takes off with some fuckin' rich dude . . . good thing, too . . . might have lost it with her.

Gary: She just dumped you?

Terry: More or less. Oh, she made a big fuckin' deal about me havin' a few little girlfriends on the side . . . but they didn't amount to shit. I coulda cared about her [*becoming visibly upset*].

Gary: So you did get close with her?

Terry paused for several moments. I thought I saw him bite his lower lip to fight back emotion; but the moment passed quickly as he got out of his chair, paced the room and returned to his seat.

Terry: Look. That was ancient history. The woman was no fuckin' good. She's gone . . . good fuckin' riddance.

Throughout the session the group members tried to get Terry to acknowledge the extent of his distress, but he continued to present himself as totally in control of his life and his destiny.

Several weeks later Terry's attitudes became the focal point of the group.

Arthur: Terry, what are you so uptight about today? You been one uptight young man lately.

Terry: Yeah, well it ain't no big thing. I been gettin' hassled by this bitch I been seein' lately. She's been pressurin' me real bad. Terry don't take to that approach very much.

George: What sort of pressure are you talking about?

Terry: You know, same ol' shit . . . bitch figures a guy lay down with her a few times, then she owns him. I told her it ain't gonna be that way.

Gary: So she wants a relationship and you don't?

Terry: Yeah, same ol' deal . . . but I ain't gonna fall for it, even if she does pull that "I love you, I'm gonna have your baby" crap.

Chad: Did you say baby? She's not pregnant, is she?

Terry: Who the hell knows. I ain't gonna hang around to find out. Then she'll try to hit me up for the cash to get the thing taken care of. I don't need that.

Although the group had always gone along with Terry's negativity toward women, several group members had seemed to be losing tolerance for Terry's general style. George, Chad, and Luis seemed particularly anxious and appeared ready to say something. Finally, George began.

George: Look, I need to say something here, even if it steps on some toes. Terry, I've never said anything before. . . . I understand you've been burned and everything, but sometimes your ideas are a little hard to take.

Terry: [*Smiling*] Oh yeah, how you mean?

George: It's just that you sometimes seem to treat all women like
they're no good and deserve anything you can get away with.
I'm not so sure I can go along with that all the time.
Chad: That's true, Terry. You're pretty cold sometimes.

Terry seemed somewhat thrown off balance by the surprise
feedback. Initially at a loss for words, he soon countered.

Terry: Well maybe the problem is that some of you guys are in this
totally different place—nice ladies, homes, all that good shit.
Maybe things ain't the same for the rest of us. Hell, maybe you
might end up surprised yourselves someday. I've seen a lot of real
nice situations get real fucked up, real fast.
Arthur: Listen, I know there's bad women out there, but they aren't
all that way. It ain't right to always take advantage. You gotta
grow up and meet your responsibilities.
Luis: There definitely are women who can hurt you. But you got to
treat women with respect.
Terry: Oh man, now I'm really hearin' some shit. You guys keep rap-
pin' that "women are fine" shit somewhere else. I know better.

After several minutes of unfruitful feedback, the group gave up,
and Terry remained quiet for the rest of the session; but the issue
resurfaced in the next session. The group had gotten word of Paul's
situation and was trying to sort out the implications.

Chad: Sure, I feel bad about Paul getting screwed up, but there's no
excuse for the way he did that young girlfriend of his.
George: That really pisses me off.
Arthur: Somebody's gotta get that young man's attention.

Up to this point, Terry had seemed tense and sullen, but he
couldn't resist responding to the support being given to Kristi.

Terry: What the fuck is with you guys anyway? I mean, I ain't sure where I am anymore. You guys are gettin' just like the rest of those fuckers out there that been getting all worked up about these poor helpless women. Give me a fuckin' break, will ya?

Chad: What's your big problem, Terry? I'm getting tired of your bullshit!

Terry: Well, fuck you! I don't give a shit about you or any other pussy motherfuckers! I don't need this shit!

With that, Terry stormed out of the room.

Chad: Good riddance. His crap was really getting old.

Luis: He better be careful, he's gonna get himself hurt.

The group members sat silently for several minutes. The burst of temper had introduced a level of energy and tension that several found very unsettling. Each man seemed to have his own way of trying to cool down before speaking.

George: Look, I'm as tired of Terry's attitude as anybody; but I think that he's just like all of us. Inside he's got a lot of pain that's tearing him up.

Chad: OK, fine; but how much of his crap does anybody have to listen to?

Arthur: That young man is only headin' for trouble with that view of the world.

Gary: What do you guys think we should do?

Chad: Forget him. He's hopeless.

George: Come on, Chad. You're just pissed right now. You know he's not all bad.

The group continued to strategize about how to help Terry. Everyone agreed that he wasn't as cold and heartless as he pretended, but everyone was frustrated with his defensive walls and increasingly sympathetic to those he was hurting. We'd learned enough about him to appreciate the damage inflicted by the neglect of his early environment and by the impossible relationship with his father. Sexual exploitation of women was modeled to him; in fact, sex seemed to be the only contact possible between women and men.

In spite of his background, Terry apparently had tolerated enough intimacy to become emotionally attached to Cassandra. However, the early training and the fears of intimacy proved to be too big a hurdle to overcome. The failed relationship only lent further support to his belief that women are deceitful and intimacy is too risky.

Terry returned to the group three weeks later. Though he apologized for his outburst, he was completely unwilling to explore his background or the roots of his anger. He continued to participate superficially until he finally stopped attending altogether a month later.

● ● ● ●

The beliefs and habits of the Centerfold Syndrome are sometimes so ingrained that men simply cannot find a way to overcome them. Fortunately, even when initial efforts fail, men sometimes get second chances. I'm hoping to get another chance with Mike, Terry, and Paul.

7

OVERCOMING THE CENTERFOLD SYNDROME

The first step in overcoming the Centerfold Syndrome is recognizing the symptoms. The following list represents some of the multiple ways that the Centerfold Syndrome can be manifested. A man may have the Centerfold Syndrome if

He is visually obsessed with women's bodies.

He regularly gets girlie magazines such as *Playboy, Penthouse, Gallery,* or *Hustler.*

He throws out all his issues of *Sports Illustrated* except the annual swimsuit issue.

He frequents topless bars, strip shows, wet T-shirt contests, tight-fitting jeans contests, or perhaps even aerobics classes.

In the middle of a meaningful conversation with an intimate friend he cannot help but break eye contact to stare at an attractive female stranger passing by.

In conversation with a physically attractive woman he cannot avoid looking at her breasts.

A primary sexual outlet is masturbation with pictures of naked women.

His masturbatory fantasies are primarily of him watching a naked woman and never include him and a woman sharing an intimate moment.

When engaging in sex with a loved one, he frequently augments his arousal by imagining an unknown but sexually appealing woman.

He is excited by the prospect of his partner "dressing up" or playing the role of someone else (such as a French maid, a hooker, or a dominatrix).

His self-esteem needs regular bolstering by praise about his sexual performance.

He feels less manly if his sex partner doesn't orgasm or doesn't display a dramatic physical response to his lovemaking.

He is intensely interested in the number of orgasms his partner has or in how he compares with her previous lovers.

He generally avoids foreplay and afterplay during lovemaking.

He rarely engages in nonsexual touching.

He can only be comfortable being touched or comforted by a woman and cannot tolerate being touched by another man.

SUPPOSE YOU HAVE IT

If you've come this far, you've been willing to grant that there may be such a thing as the Centerfold Syndrome and that it may be having a negative impact on your life. To do this, you've already countered to some extent the pressure of those forces that wish to maintain the status quo. You've questioned the culture's denial of this problem. You've probably avoided being totally discouraged by those who insist that change is foolhardy since women and men always have been and always will be so essentially different that things must always continue as they are. It is hoped that you've also been alert to the ploys of those who want to shift the blame to women, claiming that they're the ones who enjoy tantalizing and controlling men.

Finally, you've had to avoid being duped by those who try to perpetuate the Centerfold Syndrome by aligning it with the cause of sexual freedom. For many years there's been a school of thought that holds that any challenge to soft-core pornography is automatically antisex. Those who profit from objectification and sexual exploitation of women claim that their products are "sex aids," that they *help* men be sexual. They do. *But they help men be sexual in the old-fashioned way that harms women and debases men's sexuality.* These magazines continue to teach the values of the Centerfold Syndrome. The cause of sexual freedom will be served when men choose to reject soft-core pornography and seek intimate sexuality with real women.

What do we need to get on with the process of change? First, we need to become deeply knowledgeable and respectful of the socialization processes of women and men. We need to be supportive of those women who are courageously challenging violent pornography, rape mythology, sexual harassment, and other forms of oppression of women's bodies. Some of these women see little hope for men or for improved male-female relationships in the foreseeable future; but there also are many women who are determined to eliminate oppression, who are not as outraged at men and not as pessimistic about improved relations between women and men. These women are sometimes confused, sometimes disappointed, frequently impatient, but resolutely hopeful that the situation can be substantially improved. Both groups of women are valuable allies in the struggle against the Centerfold Syndrome.

To have a real chance of success, we'll also need to be compassionate toward men and respectful of their experiences. Even though men need to be held accountable for their actions in establishing and perpetuating the sex industry, enormous numbers of men have also suffered from it. Men like Mike, Arthur, George,

Luis, Terry, Chad, Paul, and Fred have had their sexual potential hampered and in some cases seriously damaged by the sex industry and the Centerfold Syndrome.

The need for significant change in the most central aspect of men's lives cannot help but be terrifying. It's natural to worry that the outcome could be calamitous, that sexuality will be screwed up forever, that all that was good will be destroyed. It takes a little honest examination of the matter to acknowledge that *male sexuality is already quite screwed up.* The changes we are working toward will produce not one ounce of lost pleasure. What will be lost is a very large measure of anxiety, guilt, insecurity, alienation, and profound estrangement between women and men brought on by the current construction of male sexuality. What will be lost is sex between people who don't know or care about each other; sex between persons and objects; sex based on revenge, proving oneself, or showing off; and sex that's part of a masquerade.

THE GOALS WE PURSUE

We hear a lot of calls to give up things we like because they're bad for us: tasteless humor, cigarettes, cigars, alcohol, cholesterol, saturated fat, salt, and sugar. The last thing men need now is someone suggesting that they should do away with the "best" parts of male sexuality: no more girl watching, no more magazines, no more recreational sex.

This book is not about eliminating male sexuality; it is about overhauling it. It's about replacing irresponsible, detached, compulsive, and alienated sexuality with a sexuality that is ethically responsible, compassionate for the well-being of participants, and sexually empowering of men. To accomplish this goal we'll need to modify what we expect of women and men. Men will need to value women not only for their physical attractiveness, but also for their personal strengths, talents, and intelligence. Society's models of competent men will also need to evolve. The old idea of judging masculinity by the capacity to "score" will need to be replaced with the concept of men as sensitive and understanding. Men will need to question the idea that their manhood must be proven and regularly measured by their acquisitions and symbols of success. We must grasp the idea that many men can be more by doing less. We can help men be more fulfilled when we can help them give up the need to always be in the driver's seat (literally and figuratively), and to more frequently go along for the ride, enjoying the scenery, talking to the kids, supporting the work and appreciating the talents of the woman who's driving.

Finally, we need very different metaphors for male sexual arousal. Men's sexual arousal was once thought of as a volcanic force, a boiler of continually building pressure. Deprived of outlet, it could erupt or explode, wrecking havoc on those so foolish as to ignore its urgent needs and destructive potential. We need to replace this image of male sexual arousal with one that is both more physiologically and psychologically accurate, and more likely to generate humane approaches to sex. Sexual arousal does not endlessly mount until a man explodes. Sure, there may be wet dreams, but that's about the "worst" that can happen. Men need to learn to think of their sexual arousal as a naturally rhythmic and cyclical variation in their lives. At times they will be aroused, but if the situation is inopportune, the arousal will pass. This latter model gives men a far more useful way to think of sex—as less an irresistible demonic force and more a natural rhythm that can be integrated with the other rhythms of their lives.

HOW MEN CAN CHANGE THEMSELVES

Efforts to overcome the Centerfold Syndrome can be launched at many levels. The first of these is the level of the individual man, since short of immediate and sweeping social upheaval, there's no real likelihood that things will change unless many individual men take on this project.

The following directions are addressed to the men reading this book.

Self-Evaluation

The first step in an action plan is a careful self-evaluation: Does the Centerfold Syndrome apply to me? I'd encourage you to approach the evaluation with an open mind and not think of the Centerfold Syndrome as a rare sexual perversion. Rather, it is mainstream male sexuality—many more men have it than do not. Its features are so common to men that it's probably easier not to waste time wondering if you have it and to save your energy for figuring out exactly which aspects of it apply to you. It's certainly possible that you may have escaped the effects of mainstream male socialization, or that at some point you recognized the syndrome's symptoms and rejected it as silly and inappropriate. If so, you are in the minority.

The first step in self-evaluation is checking the symptom list to see how many items are part of your sexual behavior pattern. If you're not sure, then monitor yourself for two weeks. Pay close attention to *how* and *how much* you look at women's bodies. When you're in environments where there are large numbers of attractive women, do you frequently (several times per hour) catch yourself staring at a woman's body? Do you find yourself undressing her or trying to picture her without clothes on? Do you ever get caught looking and try to pretend you're looking at something else? Have you gone so far as to try to find secret ways to steal glances? Do these voyeuristic activities ever get in the way of your daily objectives? Do they take just a few seconds, or do they consume a sizable portion of your day?

You next might want to monitor how your voyeuristic habits affect you. Do they create emotional and physical arousal? If so, does that arousal assist or hinder completion of your daily activities? Does looking at these women ever leave you feeling tense or disoriented? Do the feelings you experience pass quickly, or do they linger throughout the day? What are your thoughts during periods of sexual arousal? Are they respectful of your partner and empowering of you? Do your thoughts treat her as a valid and integral part of your life, or do they treat her as an object?

If you can't tell for sure whether you're voyeuristic, you might consider asking a woman you know and trust. "Do you see me as someone who watches women? Who looks at women sexually? Who stares at women's body parts?" Many men are surprised to discover how much women notice.

Next, you could monitor your sexual behavior. If you masturbate (the great majority of men do), what are your principal masturbatory stimulants? Do you rely on visual stimuli, either video or pictures? Are you able to pay attention to yourself and focus on your pleasant bodily sensations, or do you focus exclusively on the characteristics of the visual image? Are you ever able to develop masturbatory fantasies that include you and a loved one together, enjoying intensely intimate pleasure, or do you exclusively fantasize about sexy strangers?

As part of your sexual evaluation, you might consider reviewing your sexual heritage. How did you learn about sex? What did you hear? How were things presented to you? How did your male peer group think about sex? How did your father? Was sex presented to you as an opportunity to be intimate with women, or as a game or holy crusade? How were sexually interested women portrayed? How were attractive women portrayed? What was a competent male supposed to be like? Where did sex fit into that formula? Spend some time reflecting on how you think of yourself as a man. Have there been a great many times when you haven't felt manly enough? Is sexual performance a critical aspect of your self-definition? How do you react to occasions of impotence? Could you survive the traumatic loss of your penis?

Think about your tolerance for intimacy. Do you allow yourself to talk openly and frankly with someone you love? After sexual intercourse, do you feel comfortable lying there and talking intimately, or do you build an emotional wall around yourself? Do you inextricably associate touch and sex? Are you comfortable being touched or embraced by a man who cares about you?

Once you have completed this self-evaluation, you should have some idea how much your sexual preferences resemble those of the

Centerfold Syndrome. You have some variant of the Syndrome if you learn that (a) you're so much into watching and objectifying women that the habits interfere with your relationships and life objectives; (b) you prefer sexual fantasies rather than the real women in your life; (c) you rely on sexual performance to feel more manly; or (d) you become so preoccupied with sexuality that sensuality, touch, and nonsexual intimacy are extremely difficult.

Recognizing the Benefits of Change

Once you've identified possible problem areas, begin to focus on the benefits of change. In what ways will a new approach to sexuality make your life less stressful and more meaningful? The list might include such items as:

Freedom from the distracting and anxiety-inducing aspects of voyeurism

Decreased reactivity to media manipulations of your attention and emotional state

Increased sense of mastery of your sexual arousal and less reactivity to sexual fetishes

Less fascination with pornography

Greater appreciation of women based on mutual interests and emotional compatibility

Less anxiety about rating your sexual performance

Greater confidence in the underpinnings of your relationships, with less possessiveness and jealousy

Greater comfort with a loved one's changing physical appearance

Greater chance for greater sexual harmony and emotional connection with your partner

Increased possibilities for nonsexual yet intimate relations with women and men

Pleasure rather than guilt and alienation after masturbation

Fewer sexual fantasies of strangers interfering with your intimate moments with a loved one

Feelings of closeness to rather than distance from your partner after sexual intercourse.

Seeing Women Differently

Once you've identified your own motivations for overcoming the Centerfold Syndrome, you can start changing your habits and behaviors. First, you'll need to do what you can to minimize the hypnotic pull produced by the culture's classical conditioning of your sexual arousal. Your conditioned arousal to sexual objects (such as leopard panties and black spike heels) and women's body parts (swelling breasts, shapely legs, curvaceous derrières) cannot just be wished away; but you *can* lessen their power over you, *and* you can develop new, more functional habits. Instead of using sexualized objects in pornography to stimulate arousal for masturbation, you can substitute more relational and emotionally meaningful fantasies. For example, instead of imagining a naked stripper or bikini-clad stranger, image yourself in an intimate, loving, and sensual setting with someone you care deeply about. Learn to focus your attention on your physical responses and pleasure, instead of on the gyrations of a sexualized object. As you learn to write your own personal "man's romance novel," you will broaden your sexual repertoire considerably and be less reliant on objectifying pornography.

You can also change the way you've learned to visually "work over" women. Once again, you can't expect to suddenly become disinterested in a "gorgeous knockout bitch in spike heels, body-hugging dress slit to her waist, heaving breasts and supple derrière slithering beneath the silky material." (I tried but couldn't squeeze any more of our conditioned sex-triggers into the description.) You *will* look. It's not a good idea to fight this, since these stimuli actually gain strength when we try to suppress them; but once the conditioned response has been elicited, you can then retake control of yourself. You don't have to stare and turn the event into a major recreational activity. You don't have to make a big exercise of mentally undressing her. Nor do you need to enhance this arousal with a stream of emotionally stimulating self-talk ("Wow, is she ever fantastic; she's the sexiest women I've ever seen; boy does she get me hot"). Instead, you can notice your response, note the beginnings of an arousal sequence, and consciously interrupt the sequence. Almost all men who have physically attractive daughters know this is possible. For them, the physical attraction is noticed, but it is stopped at that point.

You can learn to think about your sexual arousal in a different way. It's superbly ironic that we men have been taught to be masters of stoicism, utterly skilled at tolerating fear, pain, and fatigue, yet when it comes to sexual arousal we're easily overwhelmed. Lust reduces us men to weaklings. We need to think about sexual arousal in a very different way. Instead of seeing it as a powerfully urgent drive, demanding rapid expression and quick relief, we must learn to think of it as a rhythmic and natural variation, an ebbing and flowing of physical and psychological states that we can learn to integrate into our emotional and relational realities. Our sexual arousal needs to be seen not just as a physical urge, but as an integral part of our emotional, relational, and spiritual state of mind.

Finally, we can learn to "see" women differently. Instead of zooming in on body parts like a microscope, we can work to develop the capacity to see holistically. We can learn to be attracted to a broader perception of the entire woman, a perception that is less attuned to specific body features and more attuned to a global impression based on integration of input from visual, emotional, and kinesthetic senses. In that way, many standards of feminine beauty will be possible for us, as we integrate each woman's appearance into our interpersonal experience of her, rather than isolating her as a material object.

WHAT COUPLES CAN DO TO CHANGE

Although the Centerfold Syndrome affects men *and* women, it is primarily a pervasive distortion of *men's* sexuality. Therefore, men must take the bottom-line responsibility to do what they can to initiate change. Each individual man needs to assess his sexuality and acknowledge areas needing modifications. At some point, however, it can be especially useful to include one's intimate partner in the change process. Of all forms of interpersonal communication, sexual intimacy is the most complex, the most sensitive to the subtlest nuances, and the most affected by past miscommunications. Learning new patterns is more easily done jointly, with free-flowing dialogue about old wounds and anxieties.

Replacing Bad Habits

Lots of outstanding material for couples is already available. Books are plentiful for relationship building, improving marital communication, and enhancing sexual functioning. For example, Bernard Zilbergeld's *The New Male Sexuality*, mentioned in Chapter Four, is a generally valuable book that provides a range of exercises and do-it-yourself therapies for couples. Of particular relevance here are the marvelous sensate focus exercises that help couples discover sensuality and mutual pleasuring.

For men with the Centerfold Syndrome, the principal challenge will be to alter fundamentally the channels for sexual arousal—to replace the dominant role of visual stimulation with stimulation that is *also* sensual and tactile. Visual stimulation will continue to have a place, but since most men are too heavily reliant on it, it will initially need to be downplayed. Otherwise, men will never learn to develop their other sensate capabilities.

To develop new channels of sexual arousal, couples can focus on helping each other try new ways to experience pleasure. They can touch and fondle each other, openly communicating about sensations and pleasures. They can open up their sensory channels through music, massage, bathing, and hugging. To avoid maladaptive habits of emotional disconnection and stranger fantasies, a man can concentrate on looking directly into the eyes of his partner, studying her facial expressions, participating intimately in her sensual pleasure. He can learn to appreciate the subtle signs of her pleasure: goosebumps, erect nipples, rapid heart rate, or labial engorgement. He can become more attuned to the corresponding sensations in his own body—his rapid breathing or increased tactile sensitivity. Couples do well to give themselves time to participate leisurely in relearning sexual arousal, without rushing into intercourse and orgasm. Couples are also encouraged to give high priority to their intimacy needs, to make special efforts to create both psychological and physical space for relationship maintenance.

Techniques like these are invaluable in helping couples deal with sexual and emotional baggage, including the Centerfold Syndrome. The sensuality and revisualizing activities are critical components in reorienting men's sexual arousal that has previously been dependent upon voyeurism and objectification. In some ways, these exercises can be thought of as relearning, as extinguishing some old habits and replacing them with new ones.

These exercises alone, however, cannot overcome the Centerfold Syndrome. As much as this form of sensuality training can be useful, by itself it will never fly with most men. Like most forms of therapy or self-help it is unappealing to men, and will be resisted unless it is part of an overall examination of male socialization. Men and women cannot get past the Centerfold Syndrome unless they also improve their communication enough to talk openly about the damage it has done them.

Talking About the Centerfold Syndrome

Improved communication has always been an integral aspect of all efforts to enhance couple relationships, and it is critical to revamping male sexuality. Couples should make concerted efforts to understand each other's experiences and value system. This is particularly critical with the Centerfold Syndrome, since the male and female experiences are so different.

Men and women enter relationships with a lifetime of emotional baggage that they rarely discuss directly. Typically, the Centerfold Syndrome will subtly enervate the relationship, with each partner holding the other to blame. At its worst, men will blame women for not living up to centerfold beauty standards, will envy other men's "trophies," and will feel unvalidated. Women in turn will resent being seen as objects, will resent men's needs for constant masculinity reassurances, and will feel cheated out of emotional intimacy.

As a result, a primary agenda for couples is to discuss how men's sexuality has been constructed. Each partner needs to listen carefully as the other describes how voyeurism, female body worship, trophyism, validation cravings, and male fears of intimacy have affected him or her. This communication needs to be direct and honest, even when painful.

Naturally, there are prominent roadblocks to starting this communication. For one, men have usually been highly secretive about their sexual socialization, partially because they have never reflected much about it, partially because they don't want women to know the misogynistic details. It's imperative, therefore, that a man do the preliminary work mentioned earlier. Women also are reluctant to talk, partially for fear of making their partners angry, partially because they want to protect men's self-esteem in an area in which they are likely to be especially fragile.

As necessary as open communication is, it really can't stand by itself. Very few people can be expected to tear down the old sexual structure, regardless of how tattered it may be, unless there's clear evidence that a better structure is readily available. Once a couple has experienced some success in enhancing their sensuality, they will be more likely to be eager to explore matters further.

Even then, certain guidelines make things go more smoothly. First, discussions must be structured as nonjudgmental and non-blaming; neither partner is to be seen as the sole culprit, and each can be recognized as a participant in the scenario created by the culture. In this exploration of sexuality, neither blaming the other nor blaming oneself is especially helpful.

Even when taking a nonblaming posture, it's hard for a woman to hear a man reveal that he has been struggling with unhappiness over his lover not being bigger breasted, smaller hipped, or multi-orgasmic. How good can a woman feel upon hearing that her partner has envied other men? How easy can it be for a man to hear a woman's rage about being treated like an object, or to hear about her weariness of propping up his masculinity or that she has been feigning sexual responses?

Sometimes the openness required is too demanding of a couple alone. Outside counseling may be needed, or the issues may be better handled in groups of women and men. Sometimes each partner needs to do a good deal of the work individually.

One issue is abundantly clear: the emotions inherent in open confrontation with the Centerfold Syndrome are so powerful and deeply felt, they shouldn't be faced unless there is a sincere commitment to overcome this insidious malady. Such emotions are easier to deal with if the partner has made some progress and is aware of how the syndrome has been harmful to the relationship. If both the man and woman have recognized the true enemy—the Centerfold Syndrome—and have dedicated themselves to overcoming it, the sexual rehabilitation project will be both feasible and highly worthy of the effort.

WHAT A WOMAN CAN DO TO CHANGE THE MAN IN HER LIFE

When I teach my psychology of men course, the class is 75 to 100 percent women. I therefore realize that it's fairly likely that a woman is reading this book and wondering, How can I get my loved one to change? What can I do to get something started? Is there anything I can do to help him?

This is one of the most difficult questions encountered in the mental health field: How do I get someone to pay attention to a problem I am troubled about when that person doesn't see it as a problem? The issue arises frequently, of course, with alcohol abuse, and an entire support group movement—Alanon—has appeared to address the issues of concerned family members. Some Alanon principles may apply here, but let's hold that till later. It's probably best to think of the Centerfold Syndrome as a significant value difference between two people. While male sexuality can get quite dysfunctional, we must keep in mind that Centerfold Syndrome behaviors *are* socially sanctioned, and many relatively healthy men engage in these behaviors.

If you are a woman, the first step to take in addressing the Centerfold Syndrome with your partner is to assess the degree of the problem. There are several components to this. How many of the symptoms does he display? How frequently does he display them? How intense are they? Are they fairly circumscribed (that is, restricted to a narrow area of his activities), or are they broad, permeating his entire approach to life? To find answers to these questions, you might start by paying close attention to his behavior. I don't recommend any covert activities or invasions of privacy, but I do recommend being attentive and vigilant.

Pay particular attention to your sexual relationship. Does it seem to be negatively affected by his Centerfold Syndrome symptoms? How badly do these effects distress you? Are his behaviors merely an annoyance, or are they deeply troubling to you? In determining what approach to take to the problem, you must be careful to evaluate the level of your own discomfort.

Once you've gotten a sense of the severity of the problem, you are ready to approach your partner. The style of the approach is dependent upon the assessment of the problem. If the problem seems mild to relatively moderate, you can approach it as a difference of opinion—that is, a disagreement about how to structure your sexual lives. I'd consider this the "soft-line" approach. It's often best to avoid getting too far into the subject immediately, so you might begin by requesting that you and he set aside a mutually agreeable time to discuss a concern of yours. When you get together to talk, you can introduce your concern as a product of some of your recent reading and thinking. Describe to him the concept of the Centerfold Syndrome and ask his ideas about it. When you discuss this, avoid focusing only on what he does. Focus instead on how these behaviors are distressing to you.

For example, explain to him how you feel when he stares at women's bodies or brings images of naked strangers into the house. Tell him that you'd be interested in anything he'd like to share about how he became sexual, how he has learned to think about sex, what he wants sexually. Be sure to explain to him that your principal concern is to create the best possible sex life for both of you. You might even explain that you want him for yourself.

Don't expect to go far in the first meeting. Explain your concerns and ask him to give them some thought. Tell him that this book is available to him if he'd like to read the ideas firsthand. Set up a time to talk again.

What happens in the second meeting depends on what has transpired since the first. If the ideas were meaningful to him, you should have an easier time exploring the various implications of what's come up. If, however, he considers the reading confusing or nonsensical, you might try to explain why it makes sense to you. Identify the specific concerns you have and discuss them with him. For example, if he is heavily into centerfolds, explain your concerns about how that will affect his appreciation of you. If you are concerned that he stays emotionally distant, even during sex, ask him to consider sharing his thoughts with you. Keep the focus on your mismatched objectives, avoiding a direct indictment of him. To the extent that communication remains open, continue your work as a couple on your sexual relationship.

Things don't always unfold smoothly. If over a reasonable period of time your partner remains unwilling to discuss the issues with you, refusing to read the book, or generally avoiding the topic, then matters are more serious. In this case, your partner is refusing to work with you on an issue that you have defined as important. His refusal to examine the relationship becomes as critical as the original issues you identified as problematic.

Here you have a choice. How important is it for you to have a viable relationship? Is it better for you to forget the whole thing? If you don't know or can't decide, you might consider getting outside advice from a friend or professional. If you decide that the issue is important, and he continues to refuse to cooperate, you might consider a more "hard-line" approach. You might adopt an Alanon stance and refuse to enable his behavior with your silence or participation in his dysfunctional lifestyle. In extreme cases you may need to consider more extreme actions. Obviously, no major life decision should be made rashly or without consulting appropriate friends or professionals.

WHAT PARENTS CAN DO TO HELP THEIR CHILDREN OVERCOME THE CENTERFOLD SYNDROME

Though many parents find it difficult to imagine, they are in a powerful position to be influential in their children's lives. Admittedly, the global community and information superhighway are here. We no longer raise children in "The Little House on the Prairie." Daily, our homes are filled with uninvited video guests—initially only cute puppets with rubber duckies or insipid purple dinosaurs, but soon the visitors become annoying. We are introduced to whiny girls with long blonde hair who cannot function without every fashion Barbie; we meet wild-eyed hypomanic little guys whose only dream in life is to cruise intergalactic universes destroying alien starships. Many parents start by being concerned, later become despairing, and eventually throw up their hands. "Why bother, the culture is too overpowering, it's just the two of us (and we don't really agree very often)." Eventually, many discouraged parents turn over their living rooms and their communities to cultural agents—advertisers, schools, churches, and sports and social organizations.

But parents *can* make a big difference in their children's lives, even in times when the entire culture seems determined to rob parents of their influence. The first step, of course, is for parents to empower themselves, to make a commitment to being all that they can be. Next, they need to develop strategies about how to use their home-based influence most effectively, then consider how to extend that influence into the external communities their children will eventually enter.

It's long been said that children learn much less from what we tell them than they do from what we model. This is unquestionably true in the case of the Centerfold Syndrome. The home is a major place where children learn what women and men are supposed to be. Sure, they see other big people on TV or in day care, but their early images of their parents make a deep and lasting impression.

New Roles for Our Daughters

Several things are already working in favor of new roles for daughters. In the past three decades women have entered the public arena in ways they have never done before. Young girls are exposed to role opportunities, as professionals, businesswomen, sports figures, and politicians, that were never available to their mothers. It's possible then for beauty and dependence to be less emphasized in the upbringing of girls.

Many women have redefined their sexual self-image, some have not. Some remain attached to the beauty myth, others are less attached. Most of all, however, they want men to be different, but the roles for men are changing much more slowly than the roles for women. As I've already demonstrated, the sexual values of the Centerfold Syndrome remain quite prominent in cultural images of men. Parents need to take advantage of the changes underway with women, and use them as stimulants for change in men.

New Ways of Bringing Up Boys

Mothers have a greater opportunity than ever to provide or point out new role models for their daughters. It's time for fathers to do the same for their sons. Psychologist Louise Silverstein considers contemporary American culture to be at a point at which a "redefinition of fathering" can substantially alter the lives of succeeding generations. Silverstein argues that women's greater empowerment as workers and family leaders sets the stage for men to move more fully into the roles of nurturers, caretakers, and emotional participants in the family. As men move into these roles, they will be presented with unprecedented opportunities to influence their sons. Fathers can be models of caring, compassionate men who are respectful of women and who love women for their abilities and personal qualities and not only for their bodies. They can reject all forms of exploitation of women's bodies and can discourage sexist humor. They can model men who get their self-esteem not only from their work but also from their roles as loving fathers and partners. They can encourage boys to learn to care for each other, starting a process in which they will be less dependent upon women for validation. Finally, they can start a process whereby toughness and stoicism are much less emphasized, while emotional vulnerability and tenderness are allowed.

Working Together

Parents cannot be fully effective, of course, unless they cooperate. The Centerfold Syndrome will be more easily overcome if both parents work together to counter beauty myths, macho myths, and destructive sexuality messages.

Modeling alone cannot accomplish the task, since as all parents know very well, children are exposed to multiple role models. Nevertheless, parents can be available as culture interpreters, buffers, and sounding boards. To the extent they are able to be thoroughly involved in their children's lives, they will be available to help them unravel the confusing and stressful expectations placed on them. Though straight lectures are seldom as well received as we'd like, timely observations and words of wisdom can make an enormous difference at a moment of crisis, when kids are more open to input.

Parents cannot dictate which activities their children will engage in (George and Sarah learned that), and kids have a way of asserting their independence by choosing things their parents despise. Parents need to be calm, to let their values speak for them. Rather than trying to play the role of "activity Tsar," parents generally do better to focus on creating or encouraging exciting and interesting alternative activities (those that—surprise, surprise— enhance the values they are trying to promote). Rather than rave about the decadence of MTV or Miss America pageants, it might be more effective to also promote interest in somewhat more woman-positive, new-male programs like *E.R.*, *Murphy Brown*, and *Northern Exposure*.

Parents can't always punish behaviors they don't like—such as those modeled by *Beavis and Butthead*—but they can focus on reinforcing behaviors they want to encourage. In the case of the Centerfold Syndrome, parents should try to discourage or refuse to reinforce sexist behaviors in their sons, while judiciously reinforcing behaviors that demonstrate compassion, interpersonal sensitivity, and reflective thought.

Parents can become good listeners, offering more "food for thought" and less direct advice. Most importantly, they can teach their kids to be informed and questioning consumers of what culture tries to sell them. Kids can be helped to become attentive to the values taught in music, advertising, and television programming. Values messages that are overt are far less powerful than those that remain invisible yet insidious.

Finally, parents can go into the worlds of their children. Parents who are aware of what children encounter are better prepared to counter values they question. Furthermore, when community action is needed, they are in a position to know where to focus their efforts. (The latter will be discussed more fully later in this chapter.)

WHAT MEN CAN DO TO HELP OTHER MEN

When it comes to overcoming the Centerfold Syndrome, men relating with men give us the worst of all possible worlds, but it can also give us something pretty close to the best.

Let's acknowledge it: Hasn't patriarchal male culture created and continued this manner of relating with women? Haven't men learned to ogle women while in the companionship of other men? Hasn't it been said that women's bodies are the objects that allow men to bond together? How then can men getting together with other men—that is, a group of good ol' boys—do anything except keep matters the same, maybe even make them worse?

It can, and does, happen this way. Social psychologists who have studied all-male groups have found them to be powerful socializers of men, guardians of the most cherished traditional male values. Male groups are usually organized around an activity or cause, such as the military, sports teams, civic groups, and political power groups. The rules of proper group behavior are extremely strong—joking and teasing, bragging, giving advice, and arguing are allowed. Self-disclosure, emotional intimacy, touching (except secret handshakes and slaps on the back), and admissions of fear, weakness, or vulnerability are taboo. Women, except family, are denigrated, sometimes openly, sometimes covertly. Homophobia is rampant.

These all-male groups are especially interesting in terms of men's sexuality. Sex is talked about a lot. However, most of what is said is either a flat-out lie, an exaggeration, or a sexist critique of women and their approach to sexuality. In these groups, as they are currently structured, an honest, open discussion of real sexual issues concerning men is out of the question.

New Men's Groups

Having said all this, how can I make the absurd suggestion that an all-male group could possibly help to overcome the Centerfold Syndrome? The answer is pretty straightforward. It is most generally in all-male groups that young men are given their most powerful initiation into manhood. It is therefore most logical that it is also in groups of men that these rudimentary lessons can be unlearned. But how?

Obviously, the most prevalent forms of men's groups are not up to the task. Their norms are far too fossilized and they tend to be doggedly loyal to traditional values. Instead, we seem to need groups that are radically different. We need groups that are committed to discovering a new type of masculinity, one in better harmony with contemporary times. We need groups that conduct themselves according to a different set of ground rules—that allow for admission of weakness, intimate and personal conversation, expressions of fear, anxiety, and insecurity. We need groups that allow men to care for and nurture other men. We need groups committed to better relationships with women and to a new male sexuality.

Crazy, you say? Not really. Such groups currently exist and are growing in number across the country. There are profeminist men's groups, mytho-poetic men's groups (that is, groups that focus on men's spirituality), men-in-recovery groups, groups of male survivors of sexual abuse, gay men's groups, men's consciousness-raising groups, men's rights groups, and a variety of men's therapy groups. These groups vary greatly in their structure and their ideas about what men need most, but they share a common vision: that modern manhood is in serious transition, modern men are seriously confused, and modern men's groups are seriously needed.

Personally, I see almost all men's groups as having potential benefit, particularly if they help men to do something to overturn the egregiously limited possibilities for men relating with other men. Most men are badly out of touch with one another and would benefit greatly from a chance to share distress and pain with other men.

However, though I see almost all men's groups as having potential value to the spirit and morale of participants, I'm much less sanguine about their potential to help overthrow the Centerfold Syndrome. Many men's groups, such as "Christian Men's Group Promise Keepers," have a decidedly reactionary agenda, such as to "restore traditional family values"—that is, men as family leaders and women as mothers and homemakers. In my view, the best hope for revising men's sexuality comes from groups that have a serious commitment to continued empowerment of women and corresponding role freedom for men. The traditional political structure between women and men greatly benefited from the Centerfold Syndrome, and fully intends to perpetuate it.

How Men's Groups Work

As has been demonstrated in earlier chapters, groups that allow men to explore their sexuality have considerable potential to also help them change it. This happens because groups give men certain things they can't get any other way.

First, a men's group allows men to develop a sense of universality—the realization that their role struggles are not unique. Whereas men may have been overly blameful of themselves (or their spouses) for their adjustment problems, they can come to see that the demands of masculinity are onerous for many men.

Groups also give men unusual opportunities to disclose their secrets and admit their failures. Men's terror of being seen as vulnerable or weak is mitigated as each group member becomes increasingly bold in revealing insecurities and failures. This process, which I call "participative self-disclosure," allows men to ease themselves into the water, so to speak. This process is especially useful in the area of sexuality, where men are notoriously guarded and dishonest. Despite the compelling injunctions against open discussion of sexual issues, men become exhilarated about the chance to discuss and compare notes—not in the usual bullshitting fashion, but more in keeping with long-ago secret conversations with an adolescent buddy.

Men's groups help men compare notes about socialization, about experiences with fathers, about becoming fathers, and about work successes and failures. Somewhere along the way, men come to make a startling discovery, one that can forever affect their attachment to the Centerfold Syndrome. Men discover that they can nurture and care for each other without guidance or reassurance from women. They realize that they have become overly dependent upon woman to nurture and comfort them, and too distrusting and homophobic with other men. As they learn to confront their homophobic fears, they recognize that love and sex don't have to be connected. Nonsexual love and intimacy become critical components in men's struggle against the Centerfold Syndrome.

WHAT WOMEN CAN DO

There can be no doubt that a primary force in the modern realignment of gender arrangements has been the contemporary women's movement. Since only a very out-of-touch person isn't familiar with the history, goals, and successes of the women's movement, I need to add very little here, but a few points seem relevant.

First, I reiterate, the Centerfold Syndrome's damages to men would probably never have been recognized if the women's movement hadn't already demonstrated that the social construction of women's sexuality was badly flawed. Hope for change in men is dependent upon women continuing to exert pressure on those who profit from exploitation of women's bodies.

Second, women's groups both do and do not have a role in helping men reconstruct their sexuality. To a great extent, women have done enough for men, and they've got plenty of work to continue doing for themselves. It's now men's turn. What women can do is stay abreast with what men are doing, offer moral support, and when appropriate, be available for discussions about how men and women can work together to reconstruct sexuality.

WHAT WOMEN AND MEN CAN DO TOGETHER

Sometimes there's strength, and safety, in numbers. Discussion of meaningful personal issues (and sexuality is about as meaningful and personal as issues get) in a face-to-face setting can be elating when things go well, terrifying or maddening when they don't. I once had a man tell me, "Why would I want to talk about anything meaningful with my wife? I've got to live with her." I disagree with his sentiments, but understand his masculine fear of intense discussions.

Because of the increasing realization that there are considerable differences in the way women and men approach the world, a number of educational and consciousness-raising activities have begun to appear to help women and men understand, and in some cases help them to surmount, these differing orientations. In the past, different races and ethnic groups have had considerable success in improving cross-cultural sensitivity by clarifying misunderstandings and pointing out stylistic differences. The new intergender communication workshops and programs are designed to work in much the same way to help people from differing backgrounds come to appreciate the values and concerns of others.

In some ways it seems odd to suggest this type of activity for men and women, who have lived together since the beginning of time. Yet from another perspective this makes enormously good sense, because despite their supposed familiarity with each other, women and men can be considered to inhabit different worlds. John Gray may have overstated the case in his book *Men Are from Mars, Women Are from Venus*, but he was right to recognize the major differences created by gender socialization. Deborah Tannen's *You Just Don't Understand* has also contributed to the cause of greater appreciation of gender differences.

How can intergender communication workshops and programs help? Essentially, they provide exercises in which women and men can work collectively to identify the common satisfactions and difficulties in traditional gender arrangements. Many women and men find this process alone to be helpful, since, as in the men's group activity noted earlier, it helps people recognize common issues and problems.

Ultimately, of course, these groups are especially useful when they can work toward some form of resolution of relationship impasse. Frequently, this happens. Psychologists Steven Bergman and Janet Surrey have reported considerable success with their workshops, as has psychologist James O'Neil with his Gender Role Journal Workshop, and anthropologist Riane Eisler with her Partnership Way workshops.

Can these activities help us overcome the Centerfold Syndrome? Perhaps. Sexuality is certainly a critical component of gender differences and one that can stand some alteration. These workshops can provide an inexpensive and mutually supportive environment in which to examine change potential. They can also be adapted to multiple settings, including churches, schools, and community groups.

Nothing will happen, of course, unless men are willing to be honest about their sexual attitudes and habits. It remains to be seen if they will be willing to expose their darkest secrets.

WHAT WOMEN AND MEN CAN DO
TO CHANGE THE CULTURE

Changing a culture is tricky business. It's never really obvious which aspects should be addressed first—specific individuals, prominent cultural institutions, or the overriding cultural ethos or value system. The problem is illustrated by the question, Do people shape the culture or does culture shape the people? In my view, both are true. Change advocates differ, however, in where they place their emphasis.

Changing the Culture Indirectly

Let's look at the first perspective: cultural change comes about when people are educated enough to change themselves first. This perspective is regularly espoused by those powers and institutions that wish to maintain their modus operandi and downplay their role in shaping public taste and desires. For example, television executives have long held that they give the American public exactly what it wants. Purveyors of the Centerfold Syndrome have taken a similar position, that objectification and sexualized imagery of women is really consumer-driven—that is, "they want it and we provide it for them."

I couldn't be more contemptuous of the arrogance and ethical irresponsibility implicit in this outrageous denial that advertisers, television programmers, video game distributors, rock video producers, and men's magazine publishers are major shapers of male sexual attitudes and behaviors. I acknowledge, however, that they are accurate in one respect. If men and women were to join together to speak out against the Centerfold Syndrome, matters would change very quickly and very markedly. Look at how substantively women have been able to change public consciousness *without* significant support from many women and most men. Consider the unlimited potential of large numbers of men speaking out against these profiteers with a united voice.

This *can* happen. What it will require is a high level of public awareness of the Centerfold Syndrome and of the considerable problems with contemporary male sexuality. To some extent, a new awareness is already evident, since we're seeing greater attention given to the misbehaviors of some men—sexually violent men, sexual harassers, and sexually irresponsible men. Newspapers, magazines, and television and radio talk shows have been rife with programs describing these men and the problems they create. This is an important step, but it isn't nearly enough. We need to dramatically expand this public awareness effort by broadening the focus beyond the few aberrant men to include attention to problems inherent in the sexual socialization of *all* men. We need much more attention to how normative male socialization produces the Centerfold Syndrome and contributes greatly to sexual harassment, pornography addiction, promiscuity, and nonrelational sexuality.

If we can sensitize men to the problems of the Centerfold Syndrome, we will have a national consensus for change. Men will want to act differently because they will realize that they have been living a constricting and self-defeating sexuality. Up until now, the most vigorous challenge to some aspects of the Centerfold Syndrome—protests against the objectification of women's bodies in pornography—has been led by a small number of radical feminists who have attempted to eliminate the problem through legislation. Feminist author Andrea Dworkin and law professor Catherine MacKinnon have led a strident feminist procensorship movement that has created enormous rifts among ideological allies (because of its threat to constitutionally guaranteed free speech) and has created odd alliances between feminists and conservative Christian censorship advocates.

Although I appreciate the outrage and indignation fueling Dworkin and MacKinnon's position, I believe that there's a more effective way to eliminate pornography and other manifestations of the Centerfold Syndrome. If a large-scale national effort were made to demonstrate the significant problems of the Centerfold Syndrome and how it is destructive of the sexual lives of women *and* men, we could see a fundamentally different picture emerge. Rather than wrapping themselves in the Bill of Rights, informed men would choose to start the difficult task of giving up pornography and sexual objectification of women. They would do this with dedication because they would have realized that pornography and sexual objectification of women are not in *anybody's* best interest.

Changing the Culture Directly

Let's turn now to ways to challenge head-on the cultural institutions and practices that shape men to engage in the behaviors of the Centerfold Syndrome. People *can* change the culture, but since the culture also shapes people, the most effective change strategy is one that works from both directions simultaneously to change individuals and the culture as a whole. Although I believe that censorship is not the most effective social action strategy to change the Centerfold Syndrome, I do believe that in general women and men can and should undertake social actions to change cultural institutions while they are working to change themselves.

But where should they start? Where should women and men direct their energies to change the culture's perpetuation of the Centerfold Syndrome? The national media is as good a place as any. As we know from the national reactions to television events like *Roots*, the Super Bowl, and the O. J. Simpson trial, the television reaches a lot of people very quickly. Experts have found that, between the ages of three and eighteen, the average American child watches between seven and eight thousand hours of television *commercials*. That's a phenomenal number of messages about how the world works and about how women and men are supposed to conduct themselves. What are these messages?

Recent content analysis research reveals that although there has been some change over the past two decades, television advertising continues to portray men and women in the traditional fashion. For example, women are now more likely to be seen as having an occupation, but they still are not likely to be portrayed as "experts." (More than 90 percent of commercials are narrated by male voices.) Most important, women still tend to be portrayed as sex objects. The "Swedish Bikini Team" may no longer be with us, but beer commercials are still largely populated by semiclad and seemingly empty-headed young women.

Not only is there an unending parade of stereotyped "gorgeous babe" women in commercials, but there is also a dearth of alternative ideas about female attractiveness. Although attractive men may come in many varieties, the range of women considered attractive is relatively narrow—they must be young, shapely, and not too bright. Rarely does television (or the film industry) portray older, wiser, and physically average women as particularly attractive or sexually desirable. A broadened definition of female attractiveness is both achievable and highly desirable.

Where should we turn next? How about looking at the second most influential institution in the lives of American men: the sports industry. By any reasonable standard, the American sports industry is badly out of control, and it has been allowed to run amok as a socializer and influencer of American men. At one time, sports and athletics were thought of as useful activities to help boys learn valuable skills of group cooperation, personal challenge, physical endurance, and overcoming adversity. Today sports have gone far beyond the modest role of teaching young men about life; for many men, they've become life itself. How many times have we heard fanatical coaches and rabid athletics boosters fervently preach about how football has taught young men the most important lessons in life—to always struggle to be number one, to never let your guard down, to never let the other guy see you sweat. In general, life becomes a giant athletic event with one ultimate goal: to outperform other men and win life's most valuable commodity, the "thrill of victory"—a victory that brings financial success, peer respect, and trophy women.

At their best, sports do have lots to teach young men *and young women*; but it's been a long time since sports have been expected to function at their best. At the high school and university levels, athletic budgets and athletic events nearly suffocate all other activities—the arts, scholarship, and charitable and altruistic pursuits. The values of winning at all costs, aggressing to hurt or intimidate, and "in your face" taunting to demean a fallen opponent have replaced the joys of mutual participation and demonstration of athletic skill and grace.

As they are now experienced in American culture, sports perpetuate the Centerfold Syndrome. They instill worship of big, fast, muscular, and fearless men who carry the ball and slam dunk while they simultaneously hype bare-legged, bare-midriffed, and latex-clad young women who cheer for victory or sell beer and high-performance cars. They teach young men to seek constant validation from the applause of the crowd and the affection of women cheerleaders. They teach men to treat each other's bodies as punching bags and blocking dummies, while also teaching them that any intimacy between men is outrageous and perverted.

Sports don't have to be run this way. Parents and fans can retake control of them. Athletics can return to a manner of operating in which people can learn to improve their physical capabilities without becoming obsessed with outcome and victory or being humiliated by defeat. Both women and men can participate and be on center stage. Both men and women can cheer, encourage, and support women performers. Bodies can become appreciated for their capacity to accomplish reasonable physical objectives and participate joyously in shared physical expression. They should never be disfigured by weights and steroids to achieve inhuman capacity in the obsession with victory, or be molded and shaped by endless dieting, aerobics, and plastic surgery to become a titillating sideshow for the Roman gladiatorial circus.

What next? How about the fashion industry? Clothing serves multiple purposes, including provision of warmth and protection, indication of social status, and opportunity for ornamentation and adornment. Once the fashion industry gets involved, however, clothing can take on an additional purpose: to distort women's bodies, to exaggerate differences among women, and to endlessly contrive to drape and reveal in a manner that sexually arouses men.

The Wall Street Journal recently quoted the "accessories editor" of Vogue magazine as saying that fashion in the mid 1990s emphasizes "the return of glamour. . . . Women are more vampish and seductive."

To accomplish this "vampish" look, women are now being provided with clinging dresses, the Wonderbra, and the return of stiletto heels. If ever there were a marvelous illustration of the social construction of sexual arousal, it comes in the new call for shoes that reveal "toe cleavage," that is, the cracks between the toes.

Should women be prevented from wearing "sexy" clothes? Of course not. Once again, the issue is not one of censorship, but of good sense. Women and men need to get involved and demand fashions that allow for personal expression through sensible adornment and appreciation of fabrics, colors, textures, and styles. They should not stand for being coerced into accepting fashions that are designed primarily to display women's body parts, tantalize men, and demoralize all but the smallest number of women.

In many ways, nudity might resolve many aspects of the Centerfold Syndrome. It might eliminate the paradoxical fascination and mystery that is so often used to market centerfold magazines. If everyone were naked, it would be quite difficult to make such a big deal about relatively subtle differences between people's bodies. Admittedly, our culture is a long way from endorsing this radical idea, but it seems that the concept has enough implications to make it worthy of future research and discussion.

Corporate America also might benefit from greater attention to the issues inherent within the Centerfold Syndrome. Fortunately, many business settings have taken it upon themselves to begin educating their employees about sexual harassment and rape mythology. Unfortunately, until there is greater understanding of male sexual socialization, many men hear just one message: don't *get caught* looking at or coming on to a sexually attractive co-worker. Until men understand how sexual objectification and voyeurism hurt women *and men*, sexual harassment laws will always seem designed to protect women by restricting men's basic needs.

Another important issue for corporate America, and all other arenas in which fathers are separated from their families, is the continued development of family-supportive workplace policies such as realistic paternity leave and allowances for fathers to engage in family activities. Sons raised by fathers who are present and involved are less likely to objectify and mistreat women.

The mental health and human service fields also need to embrace the implications of the Centerfold Syndrome. Intimate counseling relationships, whether practiced by psychotherapists, priests, educators, or attorneys, have significant risk of sexual exploitation when male counselors have been raised to consider sexuality from the traditional male perspective. That is, if males are taught in adolescence to take advantage of all sexual opportunities that present themselves, how can they *unlearn* that value when as professionals they become responsible for the welfare of others? Only recently have we begun to recognize the extent of sexual abuse in intimate professional relationships. While we cannot ignore the issues of the impaired professional and make excuses for such gross unethical conduct, we should nevertheless not miss the opportunity to consider how the Centerfold Syndrome sometimes makes matters worse.

Finally, scientific research must give us some help with overcoming the Centerfold Syndrome. Sex researchers must stop thinking exclusively about sexually deviant men and impotent men. Extensive research needs to be conducted into how the Centerfold

Syndrome impairs male sexuality. As I noted in the preface, even though I've chosen to use the term "syndrome," I'd like to see more extensive research into the nature and extent of this problem. Are there actually more elements than those I've identified? Are there several distinct subvarieties of the syndrome? Much still needs to be learned.

EPILOGUE

Because the Centerfold Syndrome is so deeply interwoven with the fabric of our culture, we face a formidable challenge. Some people adamantly deny that there's a problem; others claim that things cannot be changed. But *there is* a significant problem and *it can be changed*. People will need to work together on many levels. The men in my group took on the challenge, and many of them made substantial progress. Let's look in on a later session.

• • • •

Several months after the events already described, Terry, Paul, and Fred were gone. A new member, Larry, had just joined, and we hadn't gotten to know much about him yet. Chad was in crisis.

Gary: Chad, you said you had something urgent to talk about.
Chad: [*Slumping in his chair, looking despondent*] I'm afraid I . . . I may have really screwed up this time. Why in hell can't I learn?
George: What's the problem?
Chad: You guys—except you Larry—all know about my relationship with Phyllis. She's been one of the best things that's ever happened to me. Hell, I've never had a relationship like this one.
Gary: What's the deal?
Chad: Remember I've been talking about how we've had this great relationship . . . feeling close, having fun, and that stuff . . . even the sex has been great, even though I was concerned about her being a little chubby?
George: I remember. You'd said that you were trying to get past that.
Chad: I was, and I was doing pretty well . . . pretty well until about two weeks ago, that is. See, I was playing this club when some

really knockout babe with great breasts started coming on to me and. . . .

George: Oh no. Don't tell us . . . you didn't?

Chad: [*Leaning over, holding his hand to his forehead*] Why am I so weak? Boy, do I feel like shit. Phyllis doesn't really know, but she senses something isn't right.

Larry: Sorry, I'm new here. Is it okay if I ask something?

Chad: Sure, go ahead.

Larry: Well, this girlfriend doesn't know, so you don't tell her. I guess I don't see the big problem. After all, how often do chances like that come up?

All of the group members gave each other knowing looks and smiles.

George: Larry, we got a lot of catching up to do with you.

Larry looked confused.

Gary: Larry, as we said earlier, the subject of sexuality has been a major one in here. Chad has been working on a lot of issues in that area, and this has been a type of relapse for him.

Larry: Now I'm really confused. But this is sure gonna be interesting. There was something terrible about the sex?

Chad: Yeah, it really was. See, for the last several weeks I've learned to do sex differently. I'm crazy about Phyllis. Even though her body is only fair, I've had the most meaningful sexual relationship I've ever had. I care a lot about her. We know everything about each other. I've never let someone get so close. It was terrifying at first, but now I wouldn't trade it for anything.

Larry was intrigued, but still having difficulty with Chad's struggles.

Larry: Wow! But are you trying to tell me that you don't even want to be with this beautiful woman with great tits?

Chad: Oh no. I'm sure as hell not saying that. Hell, look what I did. What I'm saying is that a great body is *no big friggin' deal!* Here I was with this girl I hardly knew. She had a perfect body, but she felt really foreign to me. It was like I was in another world. I didn't care about her. She was beautiful, but not real. Partly I felt dishonest and disloyal; partly it was just eerie. What in hell am I doing here with no clothes on with somebody I don't even know the first thing about, when I could be with somebody I'm crazy about?

And so it went. Chad had lapsed into an old pattern, but in doing so had realized what he truly wanted in a sexual relationship. Every group member who knew Chad was deeply impressed by his experience. Larry was confused, but very curious.

The group helped several men make significant steps toward overcoming the Centerfold Syndrome. Each man had his own struggles, but each man's work was enhanced by the support and encouragement of the others. At its best, the group not only provoked changes in its members, it also began to send ripples into the men's families and communities. A new man was being embraced and encouraged to consider sexuality in a new way.

We are living in a culture that is undergoing sweeping changes, and men are being expected to relate to the people in their lives in fundamentally different ways. Some changes, such as new models of fathering, have come quickly. New ideas about male sexuality, however, are far more resistant to change. Voyeurism, objectification of women's bodies, trophyism, validation needs, and fears of intimacy—the Centerfold Syndrome—have been long-standing, well-entrenched features of the way men have been taught to relate to women.

But it's time to change. Some men, like Terry and Paul, are resisting these changes. Some, like Luis and Mike, are trying to change, but are encountering substantive difficulties. Some, like Larry, are just beginning to hear about the possibilities. Finally, others, like Arthur, George, Fred, and Chad, have made marked if erratic progress on the route to a new male sexuality that generates far greater harmony among men's sexual, sensual, spiritual, social, and emotional selves. We've got a long way to go, so we'd better commit ourselves to the difficult yet exhilarating task.

REFERENCES

P.70, *biological differences are few:* Money, J., & Tucker, P. (1975). *Sexual signatures.* Boston: Little, Brown, p. 3.

P.71, *religion expresses the ideals, hopes, and needs of humankind:* Tillich, P. (1967). *Systematic theology.* Chicago: University of Chicago Press, p. 11.

P.71, *Christian tradition has placed the greatest blame:* Cited in Reuther, R. (1983). *Sexism and God talk: Toward a feminist theology.* Boston: Beacon Press, p. 168.

P.74, *spoken out against such "fossilized religious authority":* Reuther, R. (1985). *Womanguides: Readings toward a feminist theology.* Boston: Beacon Press, p. 21.

P.80, *structural differences in male brains:* LeVay, S. (1993). *The sexual brain.* Cambridge, MA: MIT Press; Moir, A., & Jessel, D. (1991). *Brain sex: The real difference between women and men.* New York: Carol Publishing Group.

P.81, *many-turreted castle of speculation:* Schreiber, L. (1993). The search for his and her brains. *Glamour,* Apr. 1993, p. 276.

P.83, *sociobiology has taken on an ambitious agenda:* Wilson, E. O. (1978). *On human nature.* Cambridge, Mass.: Harvard University Press.

P.84, *sexual selection theory:* Symons, D. (1987). An evolutionary approach: Can Darwin's view of life shed light on human sexuality? In J. Geer and W. T. O'Donohue (Eds.), *Theories of human sexuality* (pp. 91–125). New York: Plenum Press.

P.86-87, *little evidence of universal human behaviors:* Fausto-Sterling, A. (1992). *Myths of gender: Biological theories about men and women.* New York: Basic Books.

P.88, *some respects in which modern man is obsolete:* Hamburg, D. (1968). Emotions in the perspective of human evolution. In S. L. Washburn and P. C. Jay (Eds.) *Perspectives on human evolution.* New York: Holt, Rinehart & Winston.

P.90, *importance of this masculine identity development:* Chodorow, N. (1978). *The reproduction of mothering.* Berkeley: University of California Press; Gilligan, C. (1982). *In a different voice.* Cambridge, Mass.: Harvard University Press.

P.90, *traumatic disruption of the holding environment:* Pollack, W. S. (1990). Men's development and psychotherapy: A psychoanalytic perspective. *Psychotherapy, 27,* 316–321.

P.91, *challenged the "sex-role identity paradigm":* Pleck, J. H. (1995). The gender role strain paradigm: An update. In R. F. Levant & W. S. Pollack (Eds.). *A new psychology of men*. New York: Basic Books, pp. 11–32.

P.91, *undercut the essential male spirit:* Bly, R. (1990). *Iron John: A book about men.* New York: Vintage Books.

P.96, *a critical new element to thinking about men and sex:* Zilbergeld, B. (1978). *Male sexuality.* New York: Bantam Books.

P.96, *the crucial process of civilization:* Gilder, G. (1973). *Sexual suicide.* New York: Bantam Books.

P.98, *the most accepted idea of sexuality:* Fracher, J., & Kimmel, M. (1987). Hard issues and soft spots: Counseling men about sexuality. In M. Scher, M. Stevens, G. Good, & G. Eichenfield (Eds.). *Handbook of counseling and psychotherapy with men* (pp. 83–96). Newbury Park, Calif.: Sage.

P.101, *Simone de Beauvoir said of men's relationships with women:* Quoted in J. Williams (1977). *The psychology of women: Behavior in biosocial context.* New York: W. W. Norton, p. 1.

P.102, *women have most commonly been viewed as:* Williams, J. (1977). *The psychology of women: Behavior in a biosocial context.* New York: W. W. Norton.

P.103, *an intermediate stage between the child and the full-grown man:* Quoted in J. Williams (1977). *The psychology of women: Behavior in a biosocial context.* New York: W. W. Norton, p. 6.

P.103, *the undeclared war on American women:* Faludi, S. (1991). *Backlash: The undeclared war against American women.* New York: Crown Publishers.

P.104, *feminists' analyses of pornography:* Brownmiller, S. (1975). *Against our will: Men, women, and rape.* New York: Bantam Books; Dworkin, A. (1981). *Pornography: Men possessing women.* New York: Putnam; MacKinnon, C. A. (1979). *Sexual harassment of working women.* New Haven, Conn.: Yale University Press.

P.105, *impossible standard of physical beauty:* Wolf, N. (1991). *The Beauty Myth: How images of beauty are used against women.* New York: William Morrow.

P.106, *the burden of "masculinity validation":* Pleck, J. (1980). Men's power with women, other men, and society: A men's movement analysis. In E. Pleck and J. H. Pleck (Eds.), *The American man* (pp. 417–433). Englewood Cliffs, N. J.: Prentice-Hall.

P.108, *Man is free, but everywhere he is in chains:* Quoted in McConaghy, M. (1987). A learning approach. In J. Geer & W. T. O'Donohue (Eds.), *Theories of human sexuality* (pp. 287–335). New York: Plenum Press.

P.108, *markedly influences the expression of sexuality:* Kinsey, A. C., Pomeroy, W. B., & Morten, C. (1948). *Sexual behavior in the human male.* Philadelphia: Saunders.

P.108, *the articulation of a sociocultural position:* Gagnon, J., & Simon, W. (1973). *Sexual conduct.* Chicago: Aldine.

P.108-109, *Sexual conduct is learned:* Gagnon, J. (1977). *Human sexualities.* Chicago: Scott, Foresman.

P.109, *female sexual behavior draws less attention:* Salter, A. (1992). Epidemiology. In W. T. O'Donohue & J. Geer (Eds.), *The sexual abuse of children* (pp. 205–215). New York: Erlbaum.

P.110, *the Masters and Johnson four-stage sexual cycle:* Masters, W. H., & Johnson, V. E. (1966). *Human sexual response.* Boston: Little, Brown.

P.112, *to the professional community, fetishism is understood:* The American Psychiatric Association. (1994). *Diagnostic and statistical manual of mental disorders (DSM-IV),* 526.

P.113, *research experimenters were able to condition men:* Rachman, S. (1966). Sexual fetishism: An experimental analogue. *Psychological research, 16,* 293–296.

P.113, *"nonliving objects":* The American Psychiatric Association. (1994). *Diagnostic and statistical manual of mental disorders (DSM-IV),* 526.

P.114, *an eight-stage model of sexuality:* Walen, S. R., & Roth, D. (1987). A cognitive approach. In J. Geer & W. T. O'Donohue (Eds.), *Theories of human sexuality* (pp. 335–362). New York: Plenum Press.

P.118, *the early stages of sexual arousal:* Masters, W. H., & Johnson, V. E. (1975). *The pleasure bond.* Boston: Little, Brown.

P.120, *"unconnected lust" and "nonrelational sexuality":* Levant, R. F. (1995). *Masculinity reconstructed.* New York: Dutton, p. 230.

P193, *"redefinition of fathering":* Silverstein, L. B. (1993). Primate research, family politics, and social policy: Transforming "cads" into "dads." *Journal of Family Psychology, 7,* 267–282.

P.200, *the major differences created by gender socialization:* Gray, J. (1992). *Men are from Mars, Women are from Venus: A Practical Guide for improving communication and getting what you want in your relationships.* New York: HarperCollins.

P.200, *greater appreciation of gender differences:* Tannen, D. (1990). *You just don't understand: Women and men in conversation.* New York: Morrow.

P.200, *reported considerable success with their workshops:* Bergman, S. J., & Surrey, J. (1992). *The woman-man relationship: Impasses and possibilities.* Working Paper #55. Wellesley, Mass.: The Robert S. and Grace W. Stone Center for Developmental Services and Studies; O'Neil, J. M. (1995). The gender roles journey workshop. In M. Andronico (Ed.). *Men in groups: Realities and insights.* Washington, D. C.: American Psychological Association Books.

P.200, *Partnership Way workshops:* Eisler, R., & Loye, D. (1990). *The partnership way: New tools for living and learning, healing our families, our communities, and our world.* San Francisco: HarperSanFrancisco.

P.202, *feminist procensorship movement:* Dworkin, A. (1981). *Pornography: Men possessing women.* New York: Putnam; MacKinnon, C. (1979). *Sexual harassment of working women.* New Haven Conn.: Yale University Press.

P.206, *fashion in the mid 1990s emphasizes:* Agins, T. (1995). *Wall Street Journal,* Jan. 20, 1995, pp. B1, B5.

RESOURCES

READINGS IN MEN'S ISSUES

MEN'S SEXUALITY

My ideas about the Centerfold Syndrome have been informed by a wide cross-section of literature about men's sexuality. The following list provides input from the biological, evolutionary, feminist, learning theory, and social constructionist perspectives.

Bancroft, J. (1987). A physiological approach. In J. Geer & W. T. O'Donohue (Eds.), *Theories of human sexuality* (pp. 411–418). New York: Plenum Press.

Blumstein, P., & Schwartz, P. (1983). *American couples: Money, work, sex.* New York: Morrow.

Brooks, G. R. (1990). The inexpressive male and vulnerability to therapist-patient sexual exploitation. *Psychotherapy: Theory, Research, Training, 27,* 344–349.

Carnes, P. (1983). *Out of the shadows: Understanding sexual addiction.* Minneapolis, Minn.: CompCare Publishers.

Denny, N. W., Field, J. K., & Quadagno, D. (1984). Sex differences in sexual needs and desires. *Archives of Sexual Behavior, 13,* 233–245.

Ellis, B. J., & Symons, D. (1990). Sex differences in sexual fantasy: An evolutionary psychological approach. *The Journal of Sex Research, 27,* 527–555.

Fracher, J., & Kimmel, M. (1987). Hard issues and soft spots: Counseling men about sexuality. In M. Scher, M. Stevens, G. Good, & G. Eichenfield (Eds.), *Handbook of counseling and psychotherapy with men* (pp. 83–96). Newbury Park, Calif.: Sage.

Gagnon, J. H., & Henderson, B. (1975). *Human sexuality: An age of ambiguity.* Boston: Educational Associates.

Note: I am indebted to James Doyle for his assistance in compiling this resource list. His book *The Male Experience* remains the best single-author reference work for understanding men.

Gagnon, J. H., & Simon, W. (1973). *Sexual conduct: The social sources of human sexuality*. Chicago: Aldine.

Geer, J., & W. T. O'Donohue, (Eds.), *Theories of human sexuality*. New York: Plenum Press.

Gross, A. (1978). The male role and heterosexual behavior. *Journal of Social Issues, 34*, 87–107.

Herold, E., Corbesi, B., & Collins, J. (1994). Psychosocial aspects of female topless behavior on Australian beaches. *The Journal of Sex Research, 31*, 133–142.

Hsu, B., and others (1994). Gender differences in sexual fantasy and behavior in a college population: A ten-year replication. *Journal of Sex and Marital Therapy, 20*, 103–118.

Knoth, R., Boyd, K., & Singer, B. (1988). Empirical tests of sexual selection theory: Predictions of sex differences in onset, intensity, and time course of sexual arousal. *The Journal of Sex Research, 24*, 73–89.

Littewa, J. (1972). The socialized penis. *Liberation, 18*(7), 61–69.

LoPiccolo, J. (1985). Diagnosis and treatment of male sexual dysfunction. *Journal of Sex and Marital Therapy, 11*, 215–232.

Masters, W. H., & Johnson, V. E. (1975). *The pleasure bond*. Boston: Little, Brown.

Money, J. (1980). *Love and love sickness: The science of sex, gender difference, and pair-bonding*. Baltimore, Md.: Johns Hopkins University Press.

Mosher, D. L., & MacIan, P. (1994). College men and women respond to X-rated videos intended for male or female audiences: Gender and sexual scripts. *The Journal of Sex Research, 31*, 99–113.

Moye, A. (1985). Pornography. In A. Metcalfe & M. Humphries (Eds.) *The sexuality of men*. London: Pluto Press.

Muehlenhard, C. (1988). "Nice women" don't say yes and "real men" don't say no: How miscommunication and the double standard can cause sexual problems. In E. Cole & E. D. Rothblum (Eds.), *Women and sex therapy* (pp. 94–108). New York: Haworth.

Muehlenhard, C., & Linton, M. A. (1987). Date rape and sexual aggression in dating situations: Incidence and risk factors. *Journal of Counseling Psychology, 34*, 186–196.

O'Donohue, W., & Plaud, J. J. (1994). The conditioning of human sexual arousal. *Archives of Human Sexual Behavior, 23*, 321–344.

Peplau, L. A., Rubin, Z., & Hill, C. T. (1977). Sexual intimacy in dating relationships. *Journal of Social Issues, 33*, 86–109.

Pope, K. S., Keith-Spiegel, P., & Tabachnick, B. G. (1986). Sexual attraction to clients: The human therapist and the (sometimes) inhuman training system. *American Psychologist, 41*, 147–158.

Rutter, P. (1989). *Sex in the forbidden zone: When men in power—therapists, doctors, clergy, teachers, and others—betray women's trust.* Los Angeles: Jeremy P. Tarcher.

Stock, W. (1988). Propping up the phallocracy: A feminist critique of sex therapy and research. In E. Cole & E. D. Rothblum (Eds.), *Women and sex therapy* (pp.23–41). New York: Haworth.

Symons, D. (1987). An evolutionary approach: Can Darwin's view of life shed light on human sexuality? In J. Geer & W. T. O'Donohue (Eds.), *Theories of human sexuality* (pp. 91–125). New York: Plenum Press.

Teifer, L. (1986). In pursuit of the perfect penis: The medicalization of male sexuality. *American Behavioral Scientist, 29*(5), 579–599.

Walen, S. R., & Roth, D. (1987). A cognitive approach. In J. Geer & W. T. O'Donohue (Eds.), *Theories of human sexuality* (pp. 335–362). New York: Plenum Press.

Washburn, S. L., & Jay, P. C. (1977). Quoted in F. A. Beach (Ed.) *Human sexuality in four perspectives* (p. 20). Baltimore, Md.: Johns Hopkins University Press.

Weinrich, J. D. (1987). *Sexual landscapes: Why we are what we are, why we love whom we love.* New York: Charles Scribner's Sons.

Zilbergeld, B. (1992). *The new male sexuality: The truth about men, sex, and pleasure.* New York: Bantam Books.

NATURE VERSUS NURTURE

In the preceding pages, I presented my arguments about the roles of "nature" and "nurture" in causing the Centerfold Syndrome. Those wishing to conduct their own literature review might consult some of the following resources.

Allen, L. S., & Gorski, R. A. (1991). Sexual dimorphism of the anterior commissure and massa intermedia of the human brain. *Journal of Comparative Neurology, 312,* 97–104.

Allen, L. S., Richey, M. F., Chai, Y. M., & Gorski, R. A. (1991). Sex differences in the corpus callosum of the living human being. *Journal of Neuroscience, 11,* 933–942.

Barash, D. (1979). *The whisperings within.* New York: Penguin.

Blier, R. (1984). *Science and gender.* Elmsford, N. Y. : Pergamon Press.

Fausto-Sterling, A. (1992). *Myths of gender: Biological theories about women and men.* New York: Basic Books.

Goldberg, S. (1973). *The inevitability of patriarchy*. New York: Morrow.

Gorski, R., Shryne, J. E., & Southam, A. M. (1978). Evidence for a morphological sex difference within the medial preoptic area of the rat brain. *Brain Research, 148*, 333–346.

Hutt, C. (1972). *Males and females*. Harmondsworth, Middlesex, England: Penguin.

Kelly, D. B. (1988). Sexually dimorphic behaviors. *Annual Review of Neuroscience, 11*, 225–251.

LeVay, S. (1993). *The sexual brain*. Cambridge, Mass.: MIT Press.

Moir, A., & Jessel, D. (1991) *Brain sex: The real difference between women and men*. New York: Carol Publishing Group.

Money, J., & Ehrhardt, A. (1972). *Man and woman, boy and girl*. Baltimore, Md.: Johns Hopkins University Press.

Reed, E. (1978). *Sexism and science*. New York: Pathfinder.

Reineke, M. J. (1989). Out of order: A critical perspective on women in religion. In J. Freeman, (Ed.). *Women: A feminist perspective* (4th ed.) (pp.395–413). Mountain View, Calif.: Mayfield Publishing.

Rosen, R. C., & Beck, J. G. (1988). *Patterns of sexual arousal: Psychophysiological processes and clinical applications*. New York: Guilford Press.

Reuther, R. R. (1974). Misogynism and virginal feminism in the fathers of the church. In R. R. Reuther (Ed.), *Religion and sexism* (pp. 150–183). New York: Simon & Schuster.

Reuther, R. R. (1985). *Womanguides: Readings toward a feminist theology*. Boston: Beacon Press.

Schreiber, L. (1993). The search for his and her brains. *Glamour*, April 1993, 234–237, 274–276.

Symons, D. (1979). *The evolution of human sexuality*. New York: Oxford University Press.

Symons, D. (1987). An evolutionary approach: Can Darwin's view of life shed light on human sexuality? In J. Geer & W. T. O'Donohue (Eds.), *Theories of Human Sexuality* (pp. 91–125). New York: Plenum Press.

Thornhill, R. (1980). Rape in Panorpa scorpion flies and a general rape hypothesis. *Animal Behavior, 28*, 57–65.

Wilson, E. O. (1978). *On Human Nature*. Cambridge, Mass.: Harvard University Press.

How Boys Learn to Be Men

If you're interested in reading some of the classics on male socialization, you might try these.

Balswick, J. O. (1988). *The inexpressive male*. Lexington, Mass.: Lexington Books.

Bly, R. (1990). *Iron John: A book about men*. New York: Vintage Books.

Brenton, M. (1966). *The American male*. New York: Coward-McCann.

David, D. S., & Brannon, R. (1976). *The forty-nine percent majority: The male sex role*. Reading, Mass.: Addison-Wesley.

Farrell, W. T. (1974). *The liberated man*. New York: Bantam Books.

Farrell, W. T. (1987). *Why men are the way they are*. New York: McGraw-Hill.

Fasteau, M. F. (1975). *The male machine*. New York: Dell.

Gerzon, M. (1982). *A choice of heroes*. Boston: Houghton Mifflin.

Goldberg, H. (1976). *The hazards of being male*. New York: New American Library.

Gould, R. (1974). Measuring masculinity by the size of a paycheck. In J. Pleck & J. Sawyer (Eds.), *Men and masculinity* (pp. 96–100). Englewood Cliffs, N. J.: Prentice-Hall.

Hartley, R. L. (1959). Sex-role pressures in the socialization of the male child. *Psychological Reports, 5*, 459–468.

Komorovsky, M. (1976). *Dilemma of masculinity*. New York: W. W. Norton.

Levinson, D., Darrow, C., Klein, E., Levinson, M., & McKee, B. (1978). *The seasons of a man's life*. New York: Knopf.

Nichols, J. (1975). *Men's liberation: A new definition of masculinity*. New York: Penguin Books.

O'Donovan, D. (1988). Femiphobia: Unseen enemy of intellectual freedom. *Men's Studies Review, 5*, 14–16.

O'Leary, V. E., & Donahue, J. M. (1978). Latitudes of masculinity: Reactions to sex-role deviance in men. *Journal of Social Issues, 34*, 17–28.

O'Neil, J. M. (1982). Gender-role conflict and strain in men's lives. In K. Solomon & N. Levy (Eds.), *Men in transition: Theory and therapy* (pp. 5–44). New York: Plenum.

Pittman, F. (1990). The masculine mystique. *Family Therapy Networker, 14*(3), 40–52.

Pleck, J. H. (1976). The male sex role: Definitions, problems, and sources of change. *Journal of Social Issues, 32*, 155–164.

Pleck, E., & Pleck, J. H. (Eds.). (1980). *The American man*. Englewood Cliffs, N. J.: Prentice-Hall.

Sattel, J. W. (1976). The inexpressive male: Tragedy or sexual politics? *Social Problems, 23*, 469–477.

Solomon, K. (1982). The masculine gender role: Description. In K. Solomon & N. Levy (Eds.), *Men in transition: Theory and therapy.* (pp. 45–76). New York: Plenum Press.

Staples, R. (1982). *Black masculinity: The black male's role in American society*. San Francisco, Calif.: The Black Scholar Press.

Tolson, A. (1977). *The limits of masculinity*. London: Tavistock.

Tschann, J. (1988). Self-disclosure in adult friendship: Gender and marital status differences. *Journal of Social and Personal Relationships, 5*, 65–81.

Tiger, L. (1969). *Men in groups.* New York: Random House.

Wilkinson, R. (1984). *American tough: The tough-guy tradition and American character.* Westport, Conn.: Greenwood Press.

Williams, J. (1977). *The psychology of women: Behavior in a biosocial context.* New York: W. W. Norton.

New Ideas of Masculinity

Here's a sampling of some of the most recent literature on changing ideas of masculinity.

Betcher, R. W., & Pollack, W. S. (1993). *In a time of fallen heroes: The re-creation of masculinity.* New York: Atheneum.

Brod, H., & Kaufman, M. (1994). *Theorizing masculinities.* Newbury Park, Calif.: Sage.

Diamond, J. (1994). *The warrior's journey home: Healing men, healing the planet.* Oakland, Calif.: New Harbinger Publications.

Doyle, J. A. (1994). *The male experience* (3rd ed.). Dubuque, Iowa: Brown.

Gerson, K. (1993). *No man's land: Men's changing commitments to family and work.* New York: Basic Books.

Hagan, K. L. (Ed.). (1992). *Women respond to the men's movement.* San Francisco: Pandora.

Keen, S. (1991). *Fire in the belly: On being a man.* New York: Bantam Books.

Kimmel, M. (1989). From pedestals to partners: Men's responses to feminism. In J. Freeman (Ed.), *Women: A feminist perspective.* Mountain View, Calif.: Mayfield.

Kupers, T. A. (1993). *Revisioning men's lives: Gender, intimacy, power.* New York: Guilford.

Levant, R. F. (1992). Toward the reconstruction of masculinity. *Journal of Family Psychology, 5*, 379–402.

Levant, R. F. (1994). *Masculinity reconstructed: Changing the rules of manhood— at work, in relationships, and in family life.* New York: Dutton.

Levant, R. F., & Pollack, W. S. (1995). *A new psychology of men.* New York: Basic Books.

Majors, R., & Billson, J. M. (1992). *Cool Pose: The dilemmas of black manhood in America.* New York: Lexington Books.

Miedzian, M. (1991). *Boys will be boys: Breaking the link between masculinity and violence.* New York: Doubleday.

Moore, D., & Leafgren, F. (Eds.) (1990). *Men in conflict.* Alexandria, Va.: American Association for Counseling and Development.

Myers, M. F. (1989). *Men and divorce*. New York: Guilford.

Pasick, R. (1992). *Awakening from the deep sleep: A practical guide for men in transition*. San Francisco: HarperSanFrancisco.

Pasick, R. (1994). *What every man needs to know*. San Francisco: HarperSanFrancisco.

Rabinowitz, F. E., & Cochran, S. V. (1994). *Man alive: A primer of men's issues*. Pacific Grove, Calif.: Brooks/Cole.

Segal, L. (1990). *Slow motion: Changing masculinities, changing men*. New Brunswick, N. J.: Rutgers University Press.

Stoltenberg, J. (1989). *Refusing to be a man: Essays on sex and justice*. Portland, Oreg.: Breitenbush Books.

Thompson, E. H. (1994). *Older men's lives*. Newbury Park, Calif.: Sage.

Williams, C. L. (1994). *Doing "women's work": Men in nontraditional occupations*. Newbury Park, Calif.: Sage.

THE NEW MEN'S STUDIES

Since the mid 1980s, increasing attention has been paid to masculinity from historical, sociological, biological, and anthropological perspectives. These are some of the most useful works.

Carrigan, T., Connell, B., & Lee, J. (1987). Toward a new sociology of masculinity. In H. Brod (Ed.). *The making of masculinities: The new men's studies*. (pp. 63–100). Boston: Allen & Unwin.

Clatterbaugh, K. (1990). *Contemporary perspectives on masculinity: Men, women, politics in modern society*. Boulder, Colo.: Westview Press.

Craig, S. (Ed.). (1993). *Men, masculinity, and the media*. Newbury Park, Calif.: Sage.

Doty, W. G. (1993). *Myths of masculinity*. New York: Crossroad Publishing.

Eisler, R. M., & Blalock, J. A. (1991). Masculine gender role stress: Implications for the assessment of men. *Clinical Psychology Review, 11*, 45–60.

Farr, K. A. (1986). Dominance bonding through the good old boys socializing group. *Sex Roles, 18*, 259–277.

Gerson, K. (1993). *No man's land: Men's changing commitments to family and work*. New York: Basic Books.

Gilmore, D. D. (1990). *Manhood in the making: Cultural concepts of masculinity*. New Haven, Conn.: Yale University Press.

Kimmel, M. S. (1987). The contemporary "crisis of masculinity" in historical perspective. In H. Brod (Ed.). *The making of masculinities: The new men's studies* (pp. 121–153). Boston: Allen & Unwin.

Kimmel, M. S., & Mosmiller, T. E. (1992). *Against the tide: Pro-feminist men in the United States, 1776–1990: A documentary history*. Boston: Beacon Press.

Levinson, D., Darrow, C., Klein, E., Levinson, M., & McKee, B. (1978). *The seasons of a man's life*. New York: Knopf.

Messner, M. (1992). *Power at play: Sports and the problem of masculinity*. Boston: Beacon Press.

Nardi, P. M. (Ed.). (1992). *Men's friendships*. Newbury Park, Calif.: Sage.

Rotundo, E. A. (1993). *American manhood: Transformations in masculinity from the revolution to the modern era*. New York: Basic Books.

Shiffman, M. (1987). The men's movement: An empirical investigation. In M. S. Kimmel (Ed.), *Changing men: New directions in research on men and masculinity* (pp. 295–314). Beverly Hills, Calif.: Sage.

Shweder, R. A. (1994, January 9). What do men want? A reading list for the male identity crisis. *The New York Times Book Review*, pp. 3, 24.

RELATIONSHIP ENHANCEMENT

Greater attention has been given recently to the new challenges of male-female relationships and the need to improve communication between the genders. These works focus exclusively on helping men and women understand each other's interpersonal style.

Bergman, S. J., & Surrey, J. (1992). *The woman-man relationship: Impasses and possibilities*. Working Paper #55. Wellesley, Mass.: The Robert S. and Grace W. Stone Center for Developmental Services and Studies.

Eisler, R., & Loye, D. (1990). *The partnership way: New tools for living and learning, healing our families, our communities, and our world*. San Francisco: HarperSanFrancisco.

Gray, J. (1990). *Men, women, and relationships: Making peace with the opposite sex*. Hillsboro, Oreg.: Beyond Words Publishing.

O'Neil, J. M., & Carroll, M. R. (1988). A gender role workshop focused on sexism, gender role conflict, and the gender role journey. *Journal of Counseling and Development, 67*, 193–197.

Tannen, D. (1990). *You just don't understand: Women and men in conversation*. New York: Morrow.

Tannen, D. (1993). *Gender and conversational interaction*. New York: Oxford University Press.

MEN IN FAMILIES

Since the mid sixties, men have been expected to dramatically change their mode of participation in family life—as workers, fathers, and marital partners. The following is a representative sampling of the rich new literature about men's new family roles.

Barnett, R. C., Marshall, N. L., & Pleck, J. H. (1992). Men's multiple roles and their relationship to men's psychological distress. *Journal of Marriage and the Family, 54*, 358–367.

Blumstein, P., & Schwartz, P. (1983). *American couples: Money, work, sex.* New York: Morrow.

Bronstein, P., & Cowan, C. P. (Eds.). (1988). *Fatherhood today: Men's changing role in the family.* New York: Wiley-Interscience.

Brooks, G. R., & Gilbert, L. A. (1995). Men in families: Old constraints, new possibilities. In R. F. Levant & W. S. Pollack (Eds.) (1995). *A new psychology of men.* New York: Basic Books.

Cowan, C. (1988). Becoming a father: A time of change, an opportunity for development. In P. Bronstein & C. Cowan (Eds.), *Fatherhood today: Men's changing role in the family* (pp. 13–35). New York: Wiley-Interscience.

DeLarossa, R. L. (1989). Fatherhood and social change. *Men's Studies Review, 6,* 1, 3–9.

Douthitt, R. A. (1989). The division of labor within homes: Have gender roles changed? *Sex Roles, 20*, 693–704.

Ehrenreich, B. (1983). *The hearts of men: American dreams and the flight from commitment.* Garden City, N. Y.: Anchor.

Gerson, K. (1993). *No man's land: Men's changing commitments to family and work.* N. Y.: Basic Books.

Gilbert, L. A. (1985). *Men in dual-career families: Current realities and future prospects.* Hillsdale, N. J.: Erlbaum.

Gilbert, L. A. (1988). *Sharing it all: The rewards and struggles of two-career families.* New York: Plenum.

Gilbert, L. A. (1993). *Two Careers/One Family: The promise of gender equality.* Newbury Park, Calif.: Sage.

Griswold, R. L. (1993). *Fatherhood in America: A history.* New York: Basic Books.

Hewlett, B. S. (1987). Intimate fathers. In M. Lamb (Ed.), *The father's role: Cross-cultural perspectives* (pp. 292–330). Hillsdale, N. J.: Erlbaum.

Hewlett, B. S. (1991). *Intimate fathers.* Ann Arbor, Mich.: University of Michigan Press.

Hewlett, B. S. (1992). *Father-child relations: Cultural and biosocial contexts.* New York: Aldine de Gruyter.

Hochschild, A. (1989). *The second shift.* New York: Viking.

Hood, J. C. (Ed.) (1993). *Work, family, and masculinities.* Beverly Hills, Calif.: Sage.

Jump, T., & Haas, L. (1987). Dual career fathers participating in child care. In

M. Kimmel (Ed.), *Changing men: New directions in research on men and masculinity*. (pp. 9–24). Newbury Park, Calif.: Sage.

Lamb, M. (1987). The emergent American father. In M. Lamb (Ed.), *The father's role: Cross-cultural perspectives* (pp. 3–25). Hillsdale, N. J.: Erlbaum.

Levant, R., & Kelley, J. (1989). *Between father and child*. New York: Viking.

Maccoby, E. E. (1990). Gender and relationships: A developmental account. *American Psychologist, 45*, 513–520.

Nordstrom, B. (1986). Why men get married: More and less traditional men compared. In R. A. Lewis & R. E. Salt (Eds.), *Men in families* (pp.31–53). Newbury Park, Calif.: Sage.

Osherson, S. (1986). *Finding our fathers: The unfinished business of manhood*. New York: Free Press.

Osherson, S. (1992). *Wrestling with love: How men struggle with intimacy with women, children, parents, and each other*. New York: Fawcett Columbine.

Pleck, J. H. (1980). Men's power with women, other men, and society: A men's movement analysis. In E. Pleck & J. H. Pleck (Eds.), *The American man* (pp. 417–433). Englewood Cliffs, N. J:. Prentice-Hall.

Pleck, J. H. (1987). American fathering in historical perspective. In M. S. Kimmel (Ed.), *Changing men: New directions in research on men and masculinity* (pp. 83–97). Beverly Hills, Calif.: Sage.

Robertson, J. M., & Verschelden, C. (1993). Voluntary male homemakers and female providers: Reported experiences and perceived social reactions. *The Journal of Men's Studies, 1*, 383–402.

Scanzoni, E. (1982). *Sexual bargaining: Power politics in the American marriage* (2nd Ed). Chicago: University of Chicago Press.

Silverstein, L. B. (1991). Transforming the debate about child care and maternal employment. *American Psychologist, 46*, 1025–1032.

Silverstein, L. B. (1993). Primate research, family politics, and social policy: Transforming "cads" into "dads." *Journal of Family Psychology, 7*, 267–282.

Stearns, P. (1991). Fatherhood in historical context: The role of social change. In F. W. Bozett & S. M. H. Hanson (Eds.), *Fatherhood and families in cultural context*. Springer Series: Focus on men (Vol. 6) (pp. 28–52). New York: Springer.

Thompson, L., & Walker, A. J. (1989). Women and men in marriage, work, and parenthood. *Journal of Marriage and the Family, 51*, 845–872.

Walker, H. (1988). Black-white differences in marriage and family patterns. In S. M. Dornbusch & M. H. Strober (Eds.), *Feminism, children, and the new families* (pp. 87–111). New York: Guilford Press.

PSYCHOTHERAPY FOR MEN

Since more men have become willing to consider psychotherapy, efforts have been made to examine the special issues of male clients. The following works merit attention.

Brooks, G. R. (1990). Psychotherapy with traditional role oriented males. In P. A. Keller & L. G. Ritt (Eds.), Innovations in clinical practice: A source book (pp. 61–74). Sarasota, Fla.: Professional Resource Exchange.

Brooks, G. R. (1991). Traditional men in marital and family therapy. In M. Bograd (Ed.), Feminist approaches for men in family therapy. New York: Haworth Press.

Brooks, G. R. (1992). Gender-sensitive family therapy in a violent culture. Topics in family psychology and counseling, 1, 24–36.

De La Cancela, V. (1986). A critical analysis of Puerto Rican machismo: Implications for clinical practice. Psychotherapy, 23, 291–296.

Erickson, B. (1993). Helping men change: The role of the female therapist. Newbury Park, Calif.: Sage.

Gilbert, L. A. (1987). Female and male emotional dependency and its implications for the therapist-client relationship. Professional Psychology: Research and Practice, 18, 555–561.

Gilbert, L. A., & Scher, M. (1987). The power of an unconscious belief: Male entitlement and sexual intimacy with clients. Professional Practice of Psychology, 8, 94–108.

Ipsaro, A. (1986). Male client-male therapist: Issues in a therapeutic alliance. Psychotherapy, 23, 257–266.

Kiselica, M. S., Stroud, J., & Rotzien, A. (1992). Counseling the forgotten client: The teen father. Journal of Mental Health Counseling, 14, 338–350.

Levant, R. F. (1990). Psychological services designed for men: A psychoeducational approach. Psychotherapy, 27, 309–315.

Meth, R. L., & Pasick, R. S. (1990). Men in therapy: The challenge of change. New York: Guilford Press.

Okun, B. F. (1989). Therapists' blind spots related to gender socialization. In D. Kantor & B.F. Okun (Eds.), Intimate environments: Sex, intimacy, and gender in families (pp. 129–162). New York: Guilford Press.

Osherson, S., & Krugman, S. (1990). Men, shame, and psychotherapy. Psychotherapy, 27, 327–339.

Pollack, W. S. (1990). Men's development and psychotherapy: A psychoanalytic perspective. Psychotherapy, 27, 316–321.

Ragle, J. D. (1993). Gender role related behavior of male psychotherapy patients. Unpublished doctoral dissertation. University of Texas, Austin.

Scher, M. (1990). Effect of gender-role incongruities on men's experience as clients in psychotherapy. *Psychotherapy, 27*, 322–326.

Scher, M., Stevens, M., Good, G., & Eichenfield, G. (Eds.) (1987). *Handbook of counseling and psychotherapy with men* (pp. 332–342). Newbury Park, Calif.: Sage.

Silverberg, R. (1986). *Psychotherapy for men: Transcending the masculine mystique.* Springfield, Ill.: Thomas.

Solomon, K. (1982). Individual psychotherapy and changing masculine roles: Dimensions of gender-role psychotherapy. In K. Solomon & N. B. Levy (Eds.), *Men in transition: Theory and therapy* (pp. 247–273). New York: Plenum Press.

MASCULINITY AND MEN'S HEALTH

Some researchers have suggested that the masculine gender role is hazardous to men's health. These works are helpful in understanding the interaction of the male gender role and men's physical well-being.

Barnett, R. C., & Baruch, G. K. (1987). Social roles, gender, and psychological distress. In R. C. Barnett, L. Biener, & G. K. Baruch (Eds.), *Gender and stress* (pp. 122–143). New York: Free Press.

Cooper, M. L., Russell, M., Skinner, J. B., Frone, M. R., & Mudar, P. (1992). Stress and alcohol use: Moderating effects of gender, coping and alcohol expectancies. *Journal of Abnormal Psychology, 101*, 139–152.

Gove, W. R., & Hughes, M. (1979). Possible cause of the apparent sex difference in physical health: An empirical investigation. *American Sociological Review, 44*, 126–146.

Harrison, J., Chin, J., & Ficcarrotto, T. (1989). Warning: Masculinity may be hazardous to you health. In M. S. Kimmel & M. A. Messner (Eds.), *Men's lives* (pp. 296–309). New York: Macmillan.

Hazzard, W. (1989). Why do women live longer than men? Biological differences. *Postgraduate Medicine, 85*, 271–278, 281–283.

Marin, P. (1991, July 8). Born to lose: The prejudice against men. *The Nation*, 46–51.

Nathanson, C. A. (1977). Sex roles as variables in preventive health behavior. *Journal of Community Health, 3*, 142–155.

Retherford, R. (1975). *The changing sex differential in mortality.* Westport, Conn.: Greenwood Press.

Skord, K. G., & Schumacher, B. (1982). Masculinity as a handicapping condition. *Rehabilitation Literature, 43*(9–10), 284–289.

Smith, M. (1983). *Violence and sport*. Toronto: Butterworth.

Verbrugge, L. M. (1985). Gender and health: An update on hypothesis and evidence. *Journal of Health and Social Behavior, 26*, 156–182.

Waldron, I. (1976). Why do women live longer than men? *Journal of Human Stress, 2*, 1–13.

Witkin-Lanoil, G. (1986). *The male stress syndrome: How to recognize and live with it*. New York: Newmarket Press.

ETHNICITY AND MASCULINITY

Although there is considerable commonality in the challenges faced by all men, some men experience their masculinity and male roles somewhat differently than those prescribed by the dominant Euro-American ethos. Men's studies scholars have just begun to study how ethnicity or minority status affects a man's sense of masculinity. The following works provide a sense of the diversity among men.

Brod, H. (1984). Work clothes and leisure suits: The class basis and bias of the men's movement. M. *Gentle Men for Gender Justice, 11*, 10–12.

Brod, H. (1988). (Ed). *A mensch among men: Explorations in Jewish masculinity*. Freedom, Calif.: The Crossing Press.

Cazenave, N., & Leon, G. (1987). Men's work and family roles and characteristics: Race, gender, and class perceptions of college students. In M. S. Kimmel (Ed.), *Changing men: New directions in research on men and masculinity* (pp. 244–262). Beverly Hills, Calif.: Sage.

De La Cancela, V. (1986). A critical analysis of Puerto Rican machismo: Implications for clinical practice. *Psychotherapy, 23*, 291–296.

Gibbs, J. T. (1988). *Young, black, and male in America: An endangered species*. Dover, Mass.: Auburn House.

Harris, S., & Majors, R. (Eds.). African-American men [Special issue]. *The Journal of Men's Studies, 1*(3), 225–231.

Majors, R., & Billson, J. M. (1992). *Cool pose: The dilemmas of Black manhood in America*. New York: Lexington Books.

Mirande, A. (1985). *The Chicano experience*. Notre Dame, Ind.: University of Notre Dame Press.

Parham, T. A., & McDavis, R. J. (1987). Black men, an endangered species: Who's really pulling the trigger? *Journal of Counseling and Development, 66*, 24–27.

Prothrow-Stith, D. (1991). *Deadly Consequences*. New York: HarperCollins.

Staples, R. (1982). *Black masculinity: The black male's role in American society*. San Francisco: The Black Scholar Press.

Walker, H. (1988). Black-White differences in marriage and family patterns. In S. M. Dornbusch & M. H. Strober (Eds.), *Feminism, children, and the new families* (pp. 87–111). New York: Guilford Press.

Williams, W. (1986). *The spirit and the flesh: Sexual diversity in American Indian culture*. New York: Beacon Press.

Zinn, M. B. (1989). Chicano men and masculinity. In M. Kimmel & M. Messner (Eds.). *Men's Lives* (pp. 87–97). New York: Macmillan.

GAY MEN

The gay male experience is very similar to, yet very different from, that of the heterosexual man. The following titles should be useful for improving one's understanding of gay men's lives.

Bigner, J. J., & Jacobsen, R. B. (1989). Parenting behaviors of homosexual and heterosexual fathers. *Journal of Homosexuality, 18*, 173–186.

Blumenfeld, W. J. (1992). *Homophobia*. Boston: Beacon Press.

Casper, V., Schultz, S., & Wickens, E. (1992). Breaking the silence: Lesbian and gay parents and the schools. *Teachers College Record, 94*, 109–137.

Clark, J. M. (1992). Men's studies, feminist theology, and gay male sexuality. *The Journal of Men's Studies, 1*, 125–155.

DeCecco, J. (Ed.). (1985). *Bashers, baiters, and bigots: Homophobia in American society*. New York: Harrington Park Press.

Duberman, M., Vicinus, M., & Chauncey, G. (Eds.). (1990), *Hidden from history: Reclaiming the gay and lesbian past*. New York: Meridian.

Gochros, J. (1989). *When husbands come out of the closet*. New York: Harrington Park Press.

Hetrick, E. S., & Martin, A. D. (1988). The stigmatization of the gay and lesbian adolescent. *Journal of Homosexuality, 51*, 163–183.

Mohr, R. D. (1992). *Gay ideas: Outing and other controversies*. Boston: Beacon Press.

CHANGING THE DARK SIDE OF MASCULINITY

The following works are useful for understanding and preventing the destructive aspects of some men's behavior.

Brooks, G. R., & Silverstein, L. B. (1995). Understanding the dark side of masculinity: An integrative systems model. In R. F. Levant & W. S. Pollack (Eds.). *A new psychology of men*. New York: Basic Books.

Funk, R. E. (1993). *Stopping rape: A challenge for men*. Philadelphia: New Society Publishers.

Hunter, M. (1990). *The sexually abused male*. Lexington, Mass.: Lexington Books.

Kimmel, M. S. (Ed.). (1990). *Men confront pornography*. New York: Crown.

Kivel, P. (1993). *Men's work: How to stop the violence that tears our lives apart*. New York: Ballantine Books.

OTHER RESOURCES

NATIONAL ORGANIZATIONS

The American Men's Studies Association (AMSA). A national organization dedicated to teaching, research, and clinical practice in the field of men's studies. For information write to AMSA, 22 East Street, Northhampton, MA 01060.

The Men's Health Network. Promotes educational campaigns, data collection, and networking about issues related to men's health and welfare. For more information contact Men's Health Network, P.O. Box 770, Washington, DC 20044–0770.

The Men's Studies in Religion Group. Assists religious studies scholars interested in men's studies issues. This group is an officially recognized group within the American Academy of Religion (AAR). For more information contact Dr. Stephen Boyd, Department of Religion, Box 7212, Wake Forest University, Winston-Salem, NC 27109.

The National Council for African-American Men (NCAAM). A national organization committed to serving the interests of African-American men. The group holds an annual conference and publishes the Journal of African-American Men's Studies. For more information contact Jacob Gordon, c/o NCAAM, 1028 Doyle Center, University of Kansas, Lawrence, KS 66045.

The National Organization of Men Against Sexism (NOMAS). A profeminist, gay-affirmative, male positive organization dedicated to ending all forms of sexism. Hosts an annual Men and Masculinity Conference. Promotes activities within task groups focused on fathering, antiviolence and antipornography issues, and men's studies. For more information contact, NOMAS, 54 Mint Street, San Francisco, CA 94103.

The Society for the Psychological Study of Men and Masculinity (SPSMM). Promotes advances in scientific and applied psychology focused on improving understanding of male behavior, developing intervention strategies, fostering empathic dialogue between genders, and advocating for public policy changes. For more information contact SPSMM, 902 South 31st Street, Temple, TX 76504.

NATIONAL MAGAZINES AND NEWSLETTERS

Changing Men. Presents articles about men's lives from an antisexist perspective. For more information contact Changing Men, 306 N. Brooks Street, Madison, WI 53715.

First Class Male. A newsletter devoted to issues of interest to male victims of sexual abuse. For more information contact William L. Sprague, 50 N. Arlington Avenue, Indianapolis, IN 46219.

Journeymen. A quarterly publication that explores the "male-positive" men's movement. For more information contact Journeymen, 513 Chester Turnpike, Candia, NH 03034.

MAN! A quarterly journal focused on building better relationships between women and men. The publication has a mytho-poetic orientation. For more information contact MAN! 1611 West Sixth Street, Austin, TX 78703.

Men As We Are. National quarterly magazine publishing poetry and writing about men and diversity. For more information contact Men As We Are Publishing, 581 Tenth Street, Brooklyn, NY 11215–4401.

Men's Council Journal. Publishes poetry, articles, and personal reflections from a mytho-poetic perspective. For more information contact Men's Council Journal, Box 4795, Boulder, CO 80306.

Men's Health Newsletter. Monthly publication aimed at improving understanding about issues affecting men's health. For more information contact Men's Health Newsletter, 33 E. Minor Street, Emmaus, PA 18098.

Men's Reproductive Health. Published by the American Public Health Associations Task Force on Men in Family Planning and Reproductive Health. Carries news about men's reproductive health, AIDS, and male sexuality. For more information contact Men's Reproductive Health, P.O. Box 661, Capitola, CA 95010.

National Men's Resource Calendar (NMRC). Contains information about events, services, workshops, cultural programs, bookstore listings, and men's studies classes. For more information contact, NMRC, P.O. Box 800-CM, San Anselmo, CA 94979.

Partners. A quarterly magazine for lesbian and gay couples. For more information contact Partners, P.O. Box 9685, Seattle, WA 98109.

Wingspan: Journal of the Male Spirit. An international journal reporting mytho-
poetic men's activities. For more information contact Wingspan, P.O.
Box 23550, Brightmoor Station, Detroit, MI 48223.

ACADEMIC JOURNALS

GLQ: A Journal of Gay and Lesbian Studies. Publishes research on experiences of
those who have been marginalized by race, ethnicity, social class, or
sexual practice. For more information contact Carolyn Dinshaw,
Department of English, University of California, Berkeley, CA 94720.
The Journal of African-American Men's Studies. The official publication of the
National Council of African-American men (NCAAM). For more
information contact Jacob Gordon, c/o NCAAM, 1028 Doyle Center,
University of Kansas, Lawrence, KS 66045.
The Journal of Men's Studies. A quarterly publication featuring scholarship in var-
ious academic fields, diverse theoretical perspectives, and different cul-
tures. For more information contact Dr. James A. Doyle, P.O. Box 32,
Harriman, TN 37748.
Masculinities. A quarterly publication that explores the meanings of manhood
in the modern world. For more information contact Guilford Publications, Journals Department, 72 Spring Street, New York, NY 10012.

SPECIALIZED RESOURCES

The following list offers a potpourri of readings, exercises, course
syllabi, and teaching resources.

August, E. R. (forthcoming) *Men's studies: A selected and annotated bibliography*.
(2nd ed.). Littleton, Colo.: Libraries Unlimited.
Duroche, L. L. (forthcoming). *Men's studies encyclopedia*. Westport, Conn.:
Greenwood Press.
Femiano, S. (1991). *Directory of men's studies courses taught in the United States
and Canada*. For more information contact Sam Femiano, 22 East
Street, Northhampton, MA 01060.
Femiano, S. *Men's Studies Syllabi*. A collection of syllabi from from more than
thirty courses representing a variety of disciplines. For more informa-
tion contact Sam Femiano, 22 East Street, Northhampton, MA 01060.
Gertner, D. M., & Harris, J. E. (1993). *Exploring masculinity: Exercises, activities,
and resources for teaching and learning about men*. (3rd ed.). Contains

dozens of experiential exercises, individual and group activities, sample workshops, syllabi, lesson plans, and bibliographies. For more information contact Douglas M. Gertner, 922 Madison Street, Denver, CO 80206.

Thompson, D. C. (1985). *As boys become men: Learning new male roles. A curriculum for exploring male role stereotyping.* New York: Irvington Publishers.

ABOUT THE AUTHOR

Gary R. Brooks received his Ph.D. from the University of Texas, Austin, in 1976. He is currently the Assistant Chief of Psychology Service at the Olin E. Teague Veterans Center in Temple, Texas. He is associate professor of psychiatry and behavioral sciences at the Texas A&M University Health Sciences Center, an adjunct faculty member at Baylor University, and instructor of men's studies at Texas Women's University. He is an executive board member of the National Organization of Men Against Sexism (NOMAS) and co-coordinator of the Society for the Psychological Study of Men and Masculinity, a division of the American Psychological Association. He has written extensively on understanding traditional men and improving familial relationships.

INDEX